Introduction to Tessellations

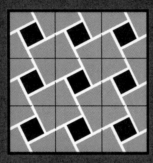

Dale Seymour and Jill Britton

DALE SEYMOUR PUBLICATIONS

Dedicated to Beverly Cory, editor par excellence.

Grateful acknowledgment is made to Cordon Art in Baarn, Holland,
exclusive worldwide representatives of the M. C. Escher heirs, for
permission to reproduce the designs of M. C. Escher in chapters 1 and 7.

Cover design: Rachel Gage
Technical illustrations: Dale Seymour

Order number DS07901
ISBN 0-86651-461-9

DALE
SEYMOUR
PUBLICATIONS
P.O. BOX 10888
PALO ALTO, CA 94303

8 9 10 11-MA-95 94

Contents

Preface   *v*

CHAPTER 1   Introduction   *1*

CHAPTER 2   Tessellating Polygons (General)   *17*

CHAPTER 3   Tessellating Polygons (Specific)   *43*

CHAPTER 4   Symmetry and Transformations   *61*

CHAPTER 5   Techniques for Generating Tessellations   *87*

CHAPTER 6   Investigations and Applications   *147*

CHAPTER 7   Creating Escher-like Tessellations   *181*

Dot Paper and Sketching Grids   *237*

Appendix: Algebraic Analysis of Regular Polygons
   Around a Point   *245*

Glossary   *247*

Bibliography   *251*

Preface

We have written this book for the layman as an introduction to the subject of tessellations. Understanding the material requires little previous background in either art or mathematics. A glossary is included to help the reader with technical terminology that may be unfamiliar.

The study of tessellations provides opportunities for exploring and discovering relationships in a creative way. Some readers may be more interested in learning about the fundamental concepts we present so that they can better analyze and describe the patterns and structure of a tessellation. Others will want this basic understanding to help them create their own pattern designs.

Numerous software programs that are available for today's personal computers enable us to draw with amazing speed and accuracy. With this new technology, we can create in just minutes or hours complex drawings that previously required days or weeks to complete. Many of the illustrations in this book were drawn with the Adobe Illustrator 88 program on the Macintosh II.

Teachers of mathematics and art may be interested in the companion book, *Tessellation Teaching Masters* by Dale Seymour (Palo Alto, CA: Dale Seymour Publications, 1989). This volume contains more than 280 full-page, reproducible illustrations, offering examples of common types of tessellations, patterns for analysis by students, designs that can be colored according to the types of symmetry represented, and grids and templates to use for sketching and tracing original designs.

For readers interested in a more rigorous and extremely comprehensive study of tessellations, we highly recommend the book *Tilings and Patterns* by Branko Grünbaum and G. C. Shephard (New York: W. H. Freeman and Company, 1987). See the bibliography for further information on this and related topics.

Readers with a particular bent for drawing Escher-like tessellations might be interested in the contest mentioned at the end of this book.

We hope you enjoy exploring tessellations. We love them, and we want to share them with you.

Dale Seymour
Jill Britton

April 1989

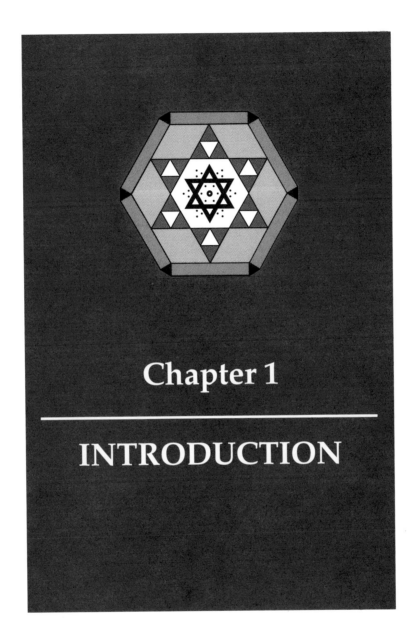

Chapter 1

INTRODUCTION

Patterns of geometric design are all around us. We see them every day, woven into the fabric of the clothes we wear, laid underfoot in the hallways of the buildings where we work, and printed on the wallpaper of our homes. Whether simple or intricate, such patterns are intriguing to the eye. In this book we will be exploring a special class of geometric patterns called *tessellations*. Our investigation will interweave concepts basic to art, to geometry, and to design.

The word *tessellation* comes to us from the Latin *tessella*, which was the small, square stone or tile used in ancient Roman mosaics. *Tilings* and *mosaics* are common synonyms for tessellations. Much like a Roman mosaic, a *plane tessellation* is a pattern made up of one or more shapes, completely covering a surface without any gaps or overlaps. Note that both two-dimensional and three-dimensional shapes will tessellate. Two-dimensional shapes may tessellate a plane surface, while three-dimensional shapes may tessellate space. In this book, when we use the word *tessellation* alone, we will always mean a plane tessellation.

Although the mathematics of tiling can become quite complex, the beauty and order of tessellations is accessible to anyone who is interested. To analyze tessellating patterns, you have to understand a few things about geometric shapes and their properties—but all you need to know is easily explained in a few pages.

We will approach this subject through directed exploration. In the first few chapters, we will be looking into the following questions: Which shapes will tessellate (that is, tile a plane without overlapping or leaving spaces)? Why will certain shapes tessellate and others not? How many different tessellating patterns can we create using two or more regular polygons? Do tessellating designs have symmetry? If so, what kind? How can we use transformations (slides, flips, and turns) to create unique tessellations? What other techniques could we use to generate these intricate designs?

Many classifications of tessellations have been established. Our explorations will focus on some of the more elementary types, including those illustrated in figures 1-1 through 1-9.

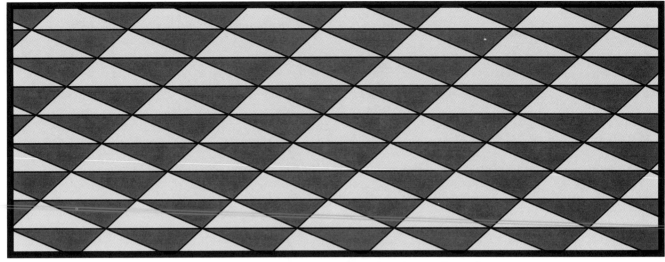

Fig. 1-1. Tessellating triangles (one shape)

Fig. 1-2. Tessellating quadrilaterals (one shape)

Fig. 1-3. Tessellating pentagons (one shape)

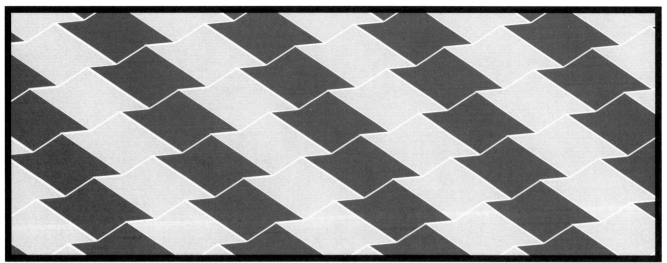

Fig. 1-4. Tessellating hexagons (one shape)

Fig. 1-5. Tessellating regular polygons (one shape)

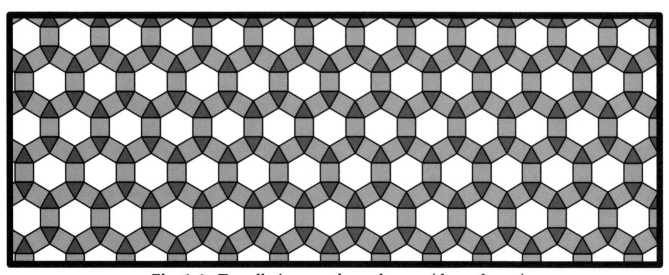

Fig. 1-6. Tessellating regular polygons (three shapes)

Fig. 1-7. Tessellating polygons (two shapes)

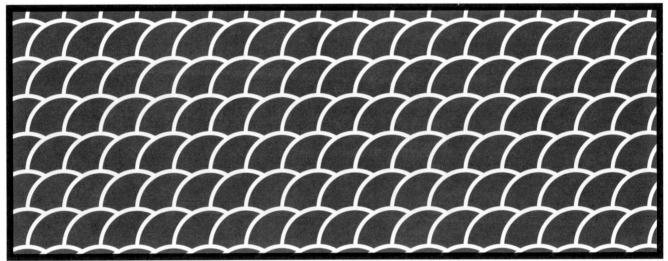

Fig. 1-8. Tessellating curved regions (one shape)

Fig. 1-9. Tessellating birds, M. C. Escher

As you can see from the preceding examples, there are many different categories of the design patterns we call tessellations. Each of the types shown will be discussed in some detail in later chapters. Regardless of the variety, however, all tessellations share one important property: they can be extended in the plane *infinitely* in every direction. There are designs that contain patterns and fill a finite space that are *not* tessellations. For all the illustrations in this book, the *infinitude* of the tessellations is assumed; it can be verified in any particular case by extending the pattern.

Fig. 1-10. A tessellation extends infinitely in all directions.

Artists, designers, and mathematicians have been interested in tessellation designs and their properties for centuries. Geometric mosaics were used as decorations as early as 4000 B.C. by the Sumerians. Archimedes (c. 287–212 B.C.) and other ancient mathematicians investigated properties of regular polygons and combinations of regular polygons that tessellated the plane. A number of polygonal tessellations were pictured in Johannes Kepler's book, *Harmonice Mundi,* published in the year 1619.

Probably the most extensive work with mosaic designs was done by Moorish artists, especially during the period 700–1500. The Islamic religion forbade artists to represent people, animals, or real-world objects in their work, limiting them to the use of calligraphy, linear designs, and geometric patterns for ornamentation. Chapter 6 explores the type of tessellating design work done by the artists of Islam and other ancient cultures, including patterns based on star polygons.

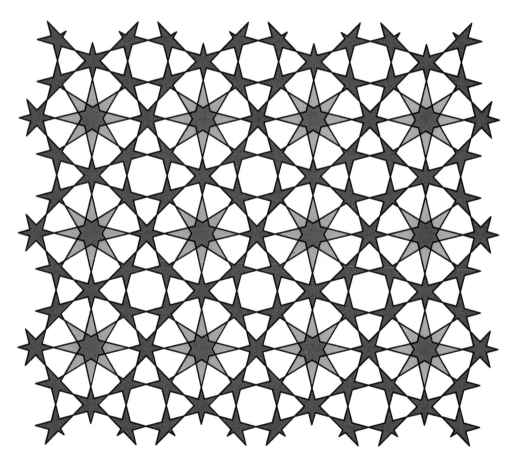

Fig. 1-11. Islamic art design

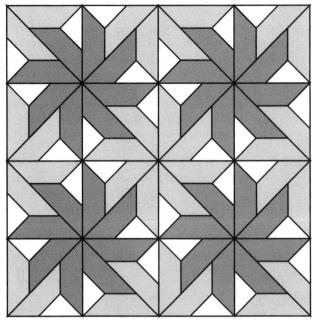

Fig. 1-12. Parquet flooring

Fig. 1-13. Parquet flooring

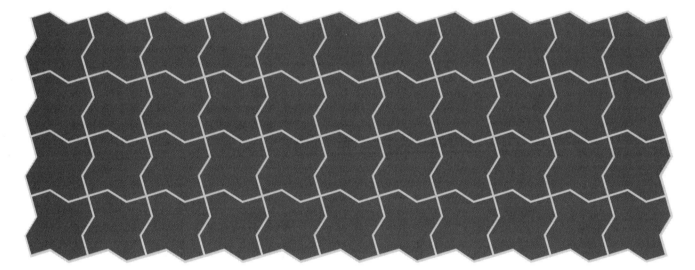

Fig. 1-14. Paving tiles

Over the centuries, artists and artisans have worked their tessellating design patterns in many different media. With mosaics of colored, glazed clay tiles, they have decorated floors, walls, and ceilings. Their tessellations have appeared on pottery, in tapestries and carpets, in metal work, in wood carvings, and in stained glass. Tessellating shapes were sometimes an integral part of the structure of an object; other times they were purely decorative additions. Some of the same designs that were used as ornamentation hundreds of years ago are still seen in modern design motifs.

Fig. 1-15. Medieval tiled flooring

Fig. 1-16. Modern linoleum pattern

Fig. 1-17. Modern ceramic tiles

Fig. 1-18. Ancient Roman mosaic floor

Fig. 1-19. Steel ceiling design (19th century)

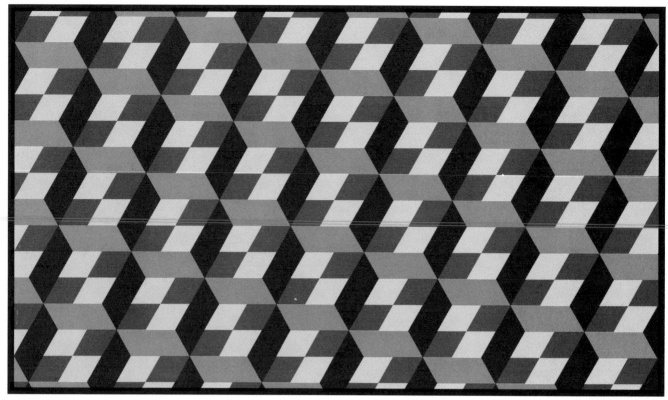

Fig. 1-20. Fabric design

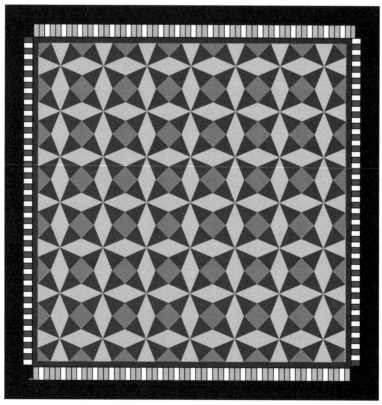

Fig. 1-21. Patchwork quilt design

Fig. 1-22. Crochet pattern

Fig. 1-23. Lace tablecloth

Fig. 1-24. Vaulting in English cathedral

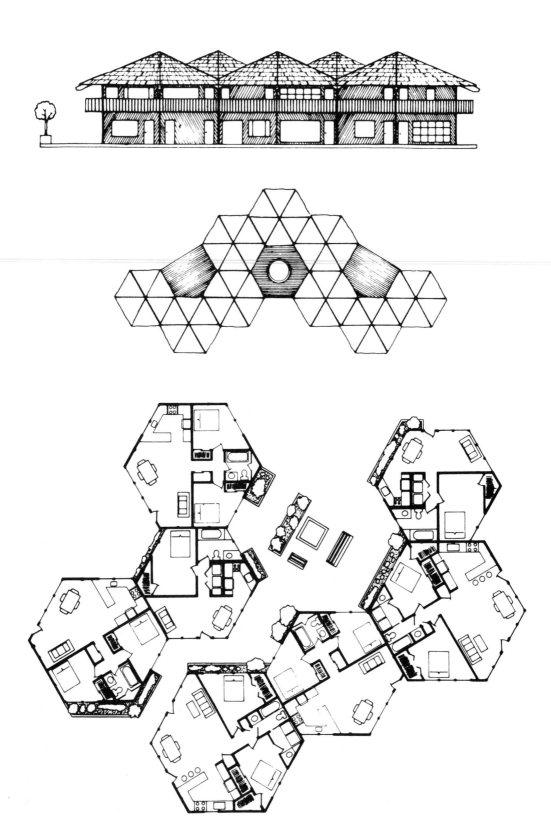

Fig. 1-25. Architectural plan for multi-unit complex using prefabricated "HEXAN" hexagonal shell units

Artisans are not the only ones to have recognized the beauty and decorative value of tessellation designs. In the twentieth century, a number of fine artists have applied the concept of tessellating patterns in their work. The best known of these is Dutch artist M. C. Escher. Inspired by the Moorish mosaic designs he saw during a visit to the Alhambra in Spain in the 1930s, Escher spent most of his life creating tessellations in the medium of woodcuts. He altered geometric tessellating shapes into such forms as birds, reptiles, fish, and people. Chapter 7 is devoted to a study of the Escher tessellations; it also introduces techniques that anyone can use to create Escher-like drawings. The fundamental properties of tessellations that we explore in chapters 2 through 6 help make Escher's work more understandable.

Fig. 1-26. *Sun and Moon,*
M. C. Escher

Fig. 1-27. Characteristic Op art design

Other contemporary artists who have used tiling patterns or modifications thereof include leading figures in the Op art movement of the 1960s. One of these is Victor Vasarely, a Hungarian-born painter working in France who created striking designs in stark black and white as well as in vibrant colors. Another is the English painter and designer Bridget Riley, whose work shows a mastery of the characteristic visual effects of Op art, with geometrically precise patterns that vibrate and flicker before our eyes.

The basis for most works of art—ancient or modern—involving tessellation patterns is an underlying grid formed by polygons. In the next chapter, we will explore different polygonal shapes to discover which ones can be used to form such a grid, or in other words, which ones tessellate the plane.

Chapter 2

TESSELLATING
POLYGONS

(General)

When we analyze a tessellation pattern, we are interested in the *closed figures,* or tiles, or tessellating shapes that form the overall design. Circles, squares, and triangles are all closed figures; each has a perimeter and an area. The simplest class of closed figures is polygons. Our purpose in this chapter is to explore different types of polygons to find out which of these shapes will tessellate. Before we begin our investigation, we will review a few basic geometric terms and concepts.

Polygon is the general classification for plane shapes with sides formed by *line segments.* A line segment is a part of a straight line, bounded by its *endpoints.* Polygons are named according to the number of sides and angles they contain, as shown in the chart below.

NAMES OF POLYGONS

SIDES AND ANGLES	NAME	SIDES AND ANGLES	NAME
3	triangle	11	undecagon
4	quadrilateral	12	dodecagon
5	pentagon	13	13-gon
6	hexagon	14	14-gon
7	heptagon	.	.
8	octagon	.	.
9	nonagon	.	.
10	decagon	n	n-gon

The sides of a polygon meet at their endpoints. These common endpoints are called *vertices* (singular, *vertex*). In figure 2-1, points A, B, C, D, E, and F are all vertices of polygon ABCDEF. Line segments are usually named by the letters that identify their two endpoints. Hence, we can say that $\overline{AB}$ is a side of the hexagon.

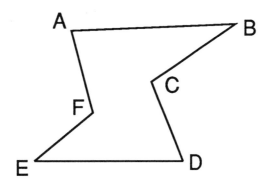

Fig. 2-1. Polygon (hexagon)

A polygon has the same number of angles as sides. When we speak of the angles of a polygon, we are referring to its *interior* angles. That is, at each vertex of the hexagon in figure 2-2, there are two angles—an interior angle and an exterior angle. Unless we specify *exterior* angle, it can always be assumed that we are referring to the interior angle.

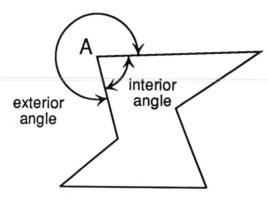

Fig. 2-2. Interior and exterior angles at point A

For convenience in discussing angles, we can name them in any of several ways, as shown in figure 2-3. Angles are often named by their vertex point only (e.g., *angle A*). If a figure is more complex, we can name the angle using a vertex and two points, one on each side of the angle (e.g., *angle CAB*), or we can use a single numeral (e.g., *angle 1*). When we use three letters to name an angle, the letter at the vertex of the angle is always named second.

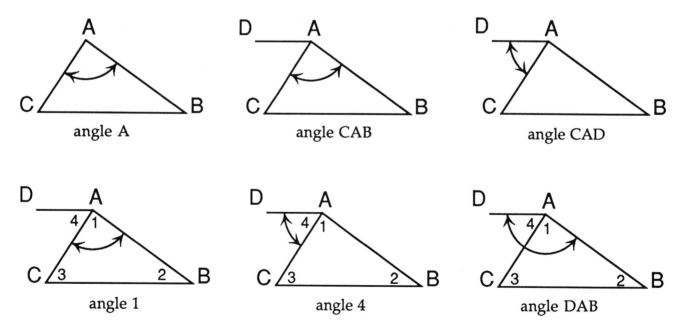

Fig. 2-3. Various ways to name angles

Angles are measured by the rotation between their sides. A complete rotation is 360 degrees (360°).

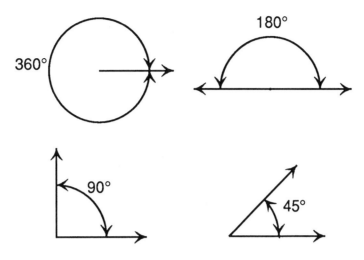

Fig. 2-4. Angle measures

We can classify angles as different types according to their measure. A complete rotation or 360° angle is called a *perigon*. This and other angle names are illustrated in figure 2-5.

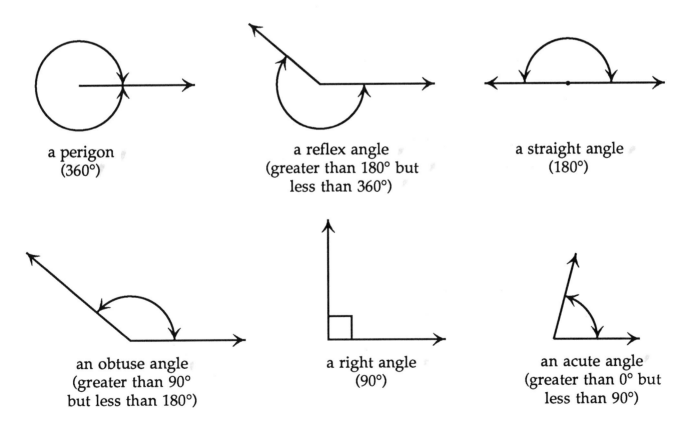

a perigon
(360°)

a reflex angle
(greater than 180° but
less than 360°)

a straight angle
(180°)

an obtuse angle
(greater than 90°
but less than 180°)

a right angle
(90°)

an acute angle
(greater than 0° but
less than 90°)

Fig. 2-5. Six types of angles

One property of the angles of a triangle is extremely important in understanding which polygons tessellate: *The sum of the interior angles of any triangle equals 180°.* We will not present a formal proof of this, but a simple demonstration will verify the relationship. After cutting a triangular shape from paper, tear off the three vertices of the triangle. When placed adjacent to each other, the three angles form a straight angle (180°).

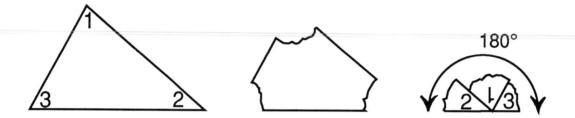

Fig. 2-6. Demonstration that the sum of the angles of a triangle equals 180°

Since a triangle is the simplest polygonal shape, we will start with the triangle in our investigation of which polygons tessellate. Also, to keep things simple, we will explore tessellating with a single triangular shape rather than combinations of different triangular shapes.

Two triangles that have the same size and shape are said to be *congruent* triangles. In figure 2-7, it's easy to see that ΔABC could be superimposed exactly on ΔDEF, so they are congruent. We write this relationship as ΔABC ≅ ΔDEF. Perhaps less obvious is the fact that triangles ABC and GHI are also congruent. We need only flip ΔGHI and then it, too, could be superimposed exactly on ΔABC.

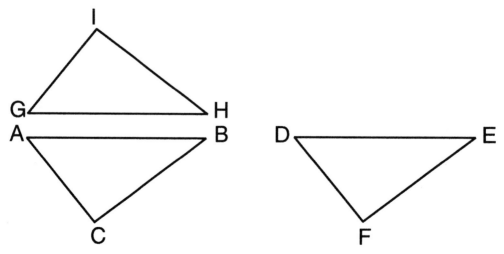

Fig. 2-7. Triangles ABC, DEF, and GHI are congruent.

We are about to explore the following questions:

Which triangles (if any) tessellate?

If some triangles tessellate, do they all?

Before we proceed with our investigation, let's look at some different types of triangles so that we can consider each type separately. Triangles are classified according to the relationships and the size of their sides and angles. Examples of each triangle type are shown in figure 2-8.

A triangle with three congruent sides is called an *equilateral* triangle. A triangle with three congruent angles is called an *equiangular* triangle. All equilateral triangles are equiangular and, conversely, all equiangular triangles are equilateral. Triangles with two congruent sides or two congruent angles are called *isosceles* triangles. Triangles with no congruent sides or angles are called *scalene* triangles.

Triangles can also be classified according to the measure of their angles. A triangle that contains three acute angles is called an *acute* triangle. If a triangle contains one right angle, it is a *right* triangle. Finally, a triangle that contains one obtuse angle is called an *obtuse* triangle.

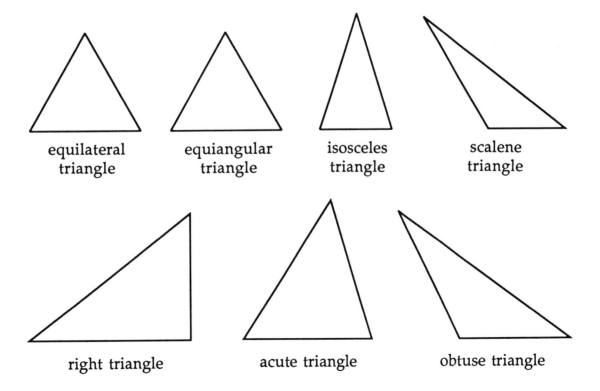

equilateral triangle equiangular triangle isosceles triangle scalene triangle

right triangle acute triangle obtuse triangle

Fig. 2-8. Seven classes of triangles

To start our investigation, let's first explore whether scalene triangles tessellate. Remember the properties of a scalene triangle: no sides congruent, no angles congruent. We might cut out a number of identical scalene triangles like the ones pictured in figure 2-9. Then we could move the triangles around on the tabletop, trying to fit them together to produce a tessellation.

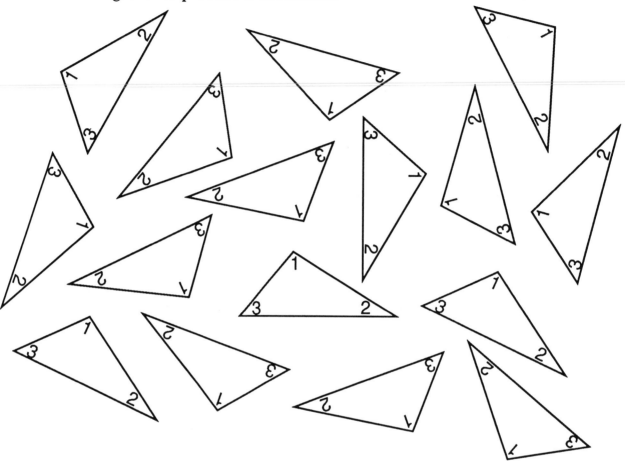

Fig. 2-9. Congruent scalene triangles: Will they tessellate?

If we position three of these triangles as shown in figure 2-10, we observe that they fit together nicely when the corresponding sides are placed together. Since the sum of the three angles is 180°, it makes sense that the three angles at point A (angles 1, 2, and 3) fill half of a complete rotation.

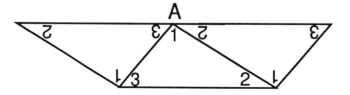

Fig. 2-10. Three congruent scalene triangles positioned to fill a half rotation

By adding three more triangles, we can completely fill all the space around the common vertex point of the six triangles. There are no gaps, no overlaps—a criterion of a tessellation.

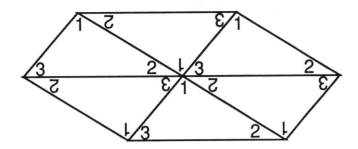

Fig. 2-11. Six congruent triangles forming a perigon (360°) with six angles

At this stage of our investigation, the question becomes: If we continue using this triangular shape, will it tessellate the plane? Figure 2-12 shows that the pattern will continue and that the scalene triangle will tessellate.

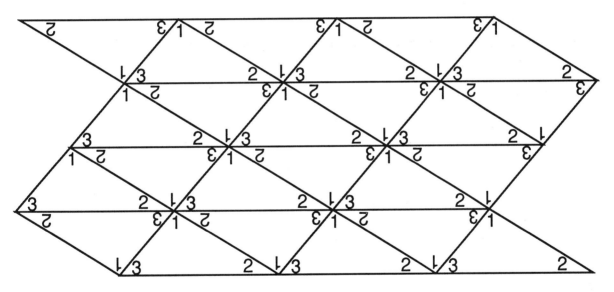

Fig. 2-12. The scalene triangle will tessellate.

Was this triangle a special case? Will all scalene triangles tessellate? Will non-scalene triangles tessellate? If you are interested in exploring these questions on your own, we encourage you to close the book at this point and do so, as discovering things independently is a rewarding way to learn. However, as a matter of expedience, we will answer these questions briefly on the following pages so that we may continue our investigation.

Fig. 2-13. Tessellating acute triangles

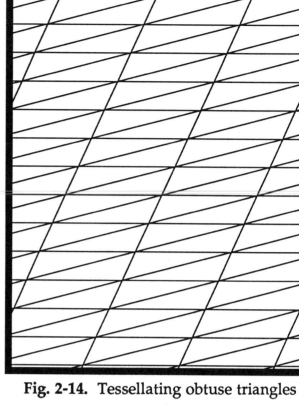

Fig. 2-14. Tessellating obtuse triangles

Fig. 2-15. Tessellating right triangles

Fig. 2-16. Tessellating isosceles triangles

Fig. 2-17. Tessellating equilateral (equiangular) triangles

Figures 2-13 through 2-17 illustrate different types of congruent triangles tessellating. You may have guessed that any triangle will tessellate the plane by itself. If so, you are right. This property is the basis for almost every type of polygonal tessellation, as you will see in the following pages. Here, then, is the first generalization we might make about tessellating polygons:

Now let's work with scalene triangles to discover the variety of interesting patterns we can create with a single triangle. If we were to cut out several congruent triangles from paper that is white on one side and red on the other side, we could create a number of different patterns.

Fig. 2-18. Opposite faces of one triangle

Placing the triangles together with the white side up, we would create a pattern like the one shown in figure 2-19. By flipping all the triangles over so that the red faces were showing, we could create a red tessellation (figure 2-20). Flipping the triangle in this way will be referred to as *reflecting* the triangle.

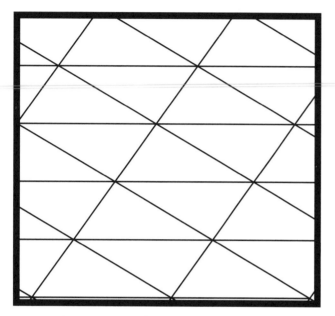

Fig. 2-19. White side tessellation

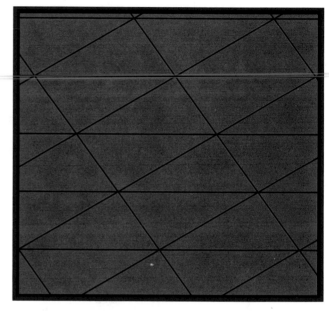

Fig. 2-20. Red side tessellation

Combining a red and a white triangle at their common edges will produce three different shapes like those shown in figure 2-21. In figure 2-22, we see the tessellation patterns that can be produced using these three different pairs of red and white triangles.

Fig. 2-21. Three ways to combine the same red and white triangles

Fig. 2-22. Three different patterns using the same scalene triangle

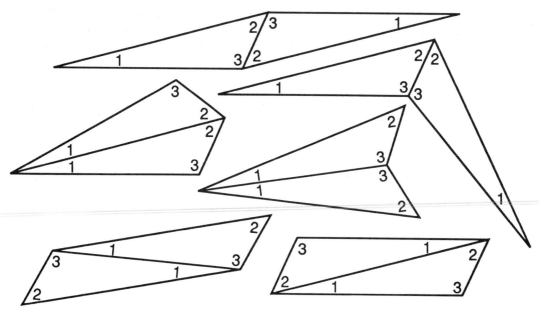

Fig. 2-23. Six different shapes formed by two congruent triangles

Now we see that not only will any triangle tessellate, but it will tessellate in different patterns depending on how the triangle edges are arranged. Shown in figure 2-23 are the six different ways we can arrange a triangle to form a tessellating pattern.

Maybe it has already occurred to you that the two triangle shapes combine in each case to form a quadrilateral. Since we will next be exploring the tessellation of quadrilaterals, we may be able to apply some information we have learned about triangles. If we view figure 2-23 again, but replace the common side with a dotted line, we see that we have six different quadrilaterals.

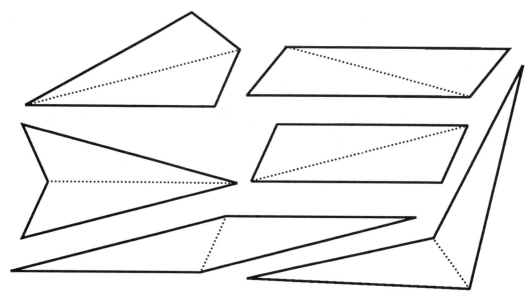

Fig. 2-24. Pairs of congruent triangles seen as quadrilaterals

Viewing pairs of triangles this way provides a nice transition into our exploration of quadrilaterals. The three patterns in figure 2-25 show us how pairs of triangles can be seen as tessellating quadrilaterals. The other three triangle pairs from figures 2-23 and 2-24 could be similarly arranged in patterns of tessellating quadrilaterals.

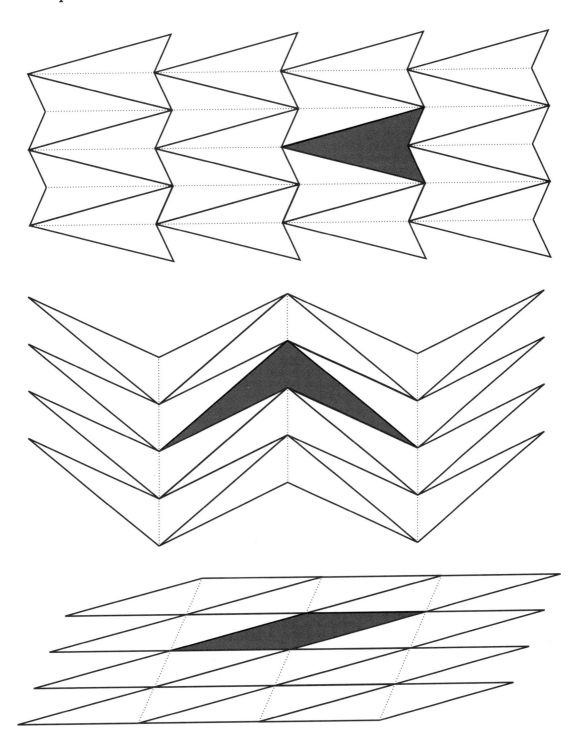

Fig. 2-25. Quadrilateral tessellations from triangle pairs

Since any triangle tessellates and in fact tessellates in six different ways when arranged as pairs that form quadrilaterals, we know that many quadrilaterals will tessellate. Recall that we began our exploration of triangles with the important fact that the sum of the interior angles of a triangle is 180°. What is the sum of the interior angles of a quadrilateral? The preceding examples, in which two triangles were combined to form a quadrilateral, give us some clues. In each case when two adjacent triangles formed a quadrilateral, their interior angles were not overlapping, nor was there any gap. From figure 2-26, we may deduce that the sum of the four angles in the quadrilateral will total two times 180°, or 360°.

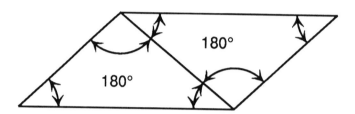

Fig. 2-26. Two congruent triangles together form a quadrilateral whose interior angles measure 360°.

Can every quadrilateral be divided into two triangles? Before we investigate this, let's review how quadrilaterals are named and classified. A quadrilateral is any four-sided polygon. Like triangles, different quadrilaterals are classified according to their special properties or the relationships of their sides and angles. Examples of the different classifications are shown in figure 2-27.

A *rhombus* is a quadrilateral with four congruent sides. A *parallelogram* is a quadrilateral with opposite sides parallel. A *rectangle* is a quadrilateral with four congruent angles (each 90°). A *square* is an equilateral rectangle. A *kite* is a quadrilateral with two pairs of adjacent, congruent sides. A *trapezoid* is a quadrilateral with only two sides parallel. A *scalene* quadrilateral is one with no sides congruent. Finally, a quadrilateral with one reflex angle (greater than 180°) is called a *concave* quadrilateral. If a polygon is not concave, then it is *convex*. Thus, the first seven shapes in figure 2-27 are all convex quadrilaterals.

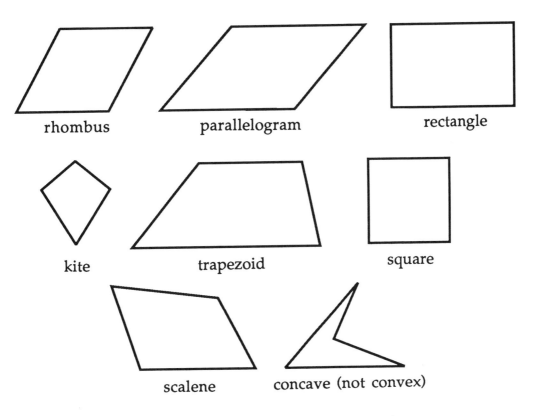

rhombus

parallelogram

rectangle

kite

trapezoid

square

scalene

concave (not convex)

Fig. 2-27. Eight classes of quadrilaterals

Now let's go back to our question: Can every quadrilateral be divided into two triangles? It is not essential that the two triangles be congruent, since every triangle's three angles total 180°. We can take a variety of quadrilaterals and divide each with a single diagonal, as shown in figure 2-28. (A *diagonal* is a line that joins the opposite vertices of a quadrilateral.) In each case, notice that the figure is divided into two triangles with no overlapping interior angles.

Fig. 2-28. Diagonals dividing quadrilaterals into two triangles

If we were to continue taking quadrilaterals of different types and drawing a single diagonal in each, this further investigation would reveal that any quadrilateral can be divided into two triangles. Therefore, the sum of the interior angles of any quadrilateral equals 360°. Cutting the four vertices off a paper quadrilateral and placing them together to form a perigon (360°) will demonstrate this property.

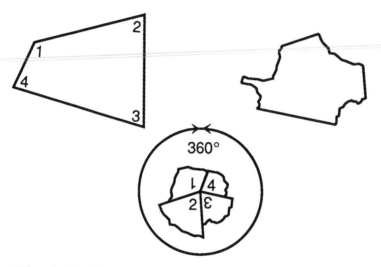

Fig. 2-29. Demonstration that the sum of the angles of a quadrilateral equals 360°

In figure 2-30, we see several congruent quadrilaterals that appear to tessellate the plane. Observe the combination of angles that are located at each vertex point. In each case, the sum of angles 1, 2, 3, and 4 equals 360°.

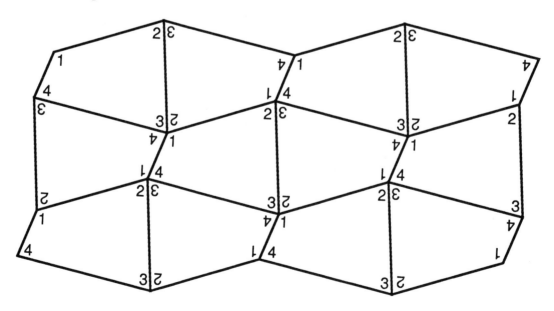

Fig. 2-30. Tessellating quadrilaterals

It might seem that *concave* quadrilaterals would *not* tessellate because of their large interior angle. However, figure 2-31 shows that even concave quadrilaterals tessellate. Notice once again that angles 1, 2, 3, and 4 all appear at each vertex.

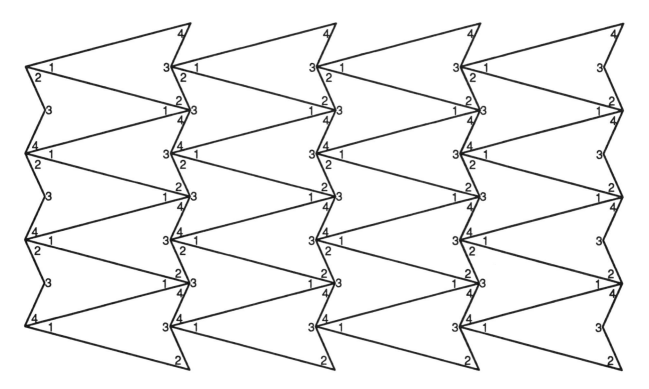

Fig. 2-31. Tessellating concave quadrilaterals

Thus we come to another generalization about tessellating polygons:

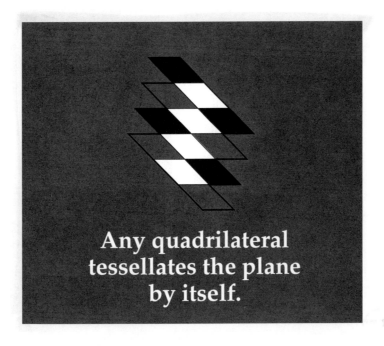

Any quadrilateral tessellates the plane by itself.

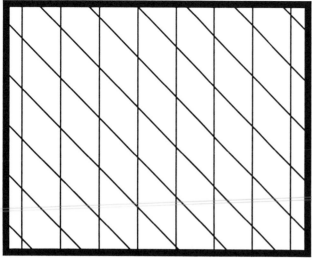

Fig. 2-32. Tessellating rhombi

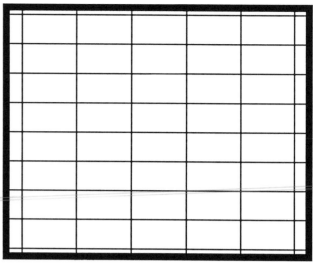

Fig. 2-33. Tessellating rectangles

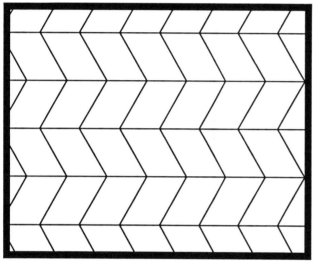

Fig. 2-34. Tessellating parallelograms

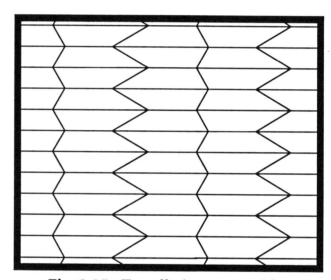

Fig. 2-35. Tessellating trapezoids

Fig. 2-36.
Tessellating scalene quadrilaterals

Fig. 2-37.
Tessellating concave quadrilaterals

Figures 2-32 through 2-37 illustrate the patterns of six different types of tessellating quadrilaterals. Recognizing that any quadrilateral will tessellate, we might then ask: Will quadrilaterals tessellate in different patterns by pairs, as triangles do? We can approach this question, as we did with triangles, by envisioning a quadrilateral cut from paper colored white on one side and red on the other. Flipping or reflecting the white shape produces the red, and vice versa.

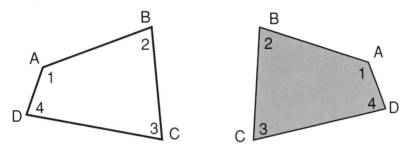

Fig. 2-38. Quadrilateral and its reflection

Using the quadrilateral pictured in figure 2-38, we know that we can form a tessellation of all white shapes, and that we can form a tessellation from all red shapes. The question is, can we form different tessellations from the red and white shapes combined? The four possible combinations of this particular quadrilateral are shown in figure 2-39.

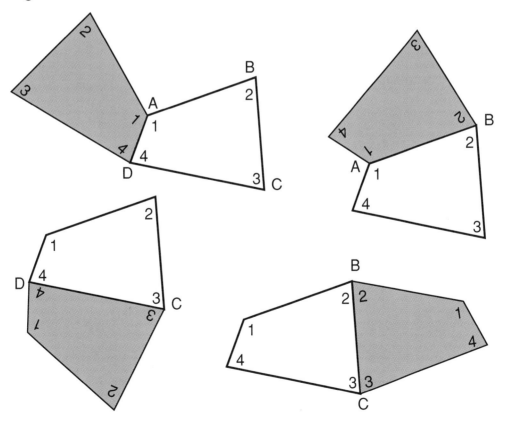

Fig. 2-39. Four ways to combine the same red and white quadrilaterals

In figure 2-39, notice that the same angle appears twice at each pair of common vertices. In all our previous examples of tessellating quadrilaterals in which no shapes were reflected, each of the four angles appeared once at the vertex point. In this new situation, where we see one angle appearing twice, we question the likelihood that a combination of the other angles would exactly fill the remaining angle space.

When we were experimenting with red and white triangles, we found that they tessellated because a pair of triangles always formed a quadrilateral (and, as we now know, all quadrilaterals tessellate). However, when we place a quadrilateral (white) and its reflection (red) together along a common side, we form a six-sided polygon, or a hexagon. It appears that the hexagons thus created may not tessellate. As we have not yet begun to investigate hexagons, we will for the time being conclude that while every quadrilateral will tessellate, a quadrilateral will not necessarily tessellate in a pattern with its reflection, as does a triangle.

Let's next investigate whether or not five-sided polygons, or pentagons, will tessellate. Once more we can begin by cutting a pentagonal shape from a piece of paper. We number the five angles, tear them off the pentagon, and observe relationships among them. A demonstration of this experiment is shown in figure 2-40. Notice that the sum of the angles is greater than 360°. Is this true of all pentagons? Does this mean that no pentagon will tessellate? Is it necessary in a tessellation that the tessellating shape have each of its angles represented at a vertex point? These are all good questions to pursue.

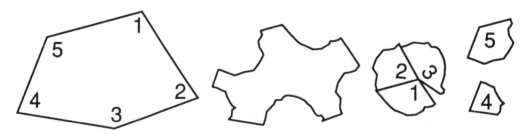

Fig. 2-40. Experiment with a paper pentagon

As we did with both triangles and quadrilaterals, we might cut out a number of congruent pentagons and try placing them in a tessellation pattern. A few such experiments would probably lead to frustration and the conclusion that at least some pentagons won't tessellate. But, some pentagons *will* tessellate.

Figures 2-41 and 2-42 show pentagonal shapes that tessellate. What special relationship do the sides of each pentagon have in figure 2-41? Could you modify figure 2-42 to make a similar tessellation with a slightly different pentagon? Draw or describe your variation.

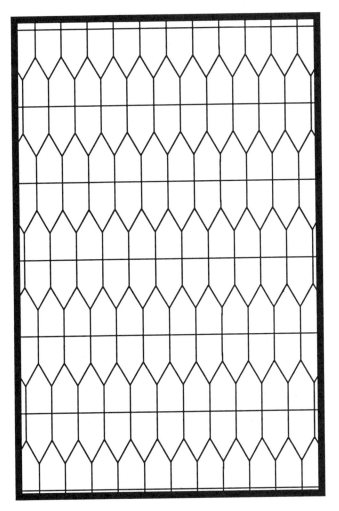

Fig. 2-41. Tessellating pentagons   **Fig. 2-42.** Tessellating pentagons

At this point we will leave our investigation of pentagons with the conclusion that some pentagons tessellate and others do not. In the next chapter, we will explore the special properties of pentagons that relate to their tessellations.

Now let's turn our attention to hexagons. The tessellation of hexagons is worthy of special consideration. We have learned that every quadrilateral tessellates, and we can observe that pairs of tessellating quadrilaterals form special hexagons. What is special about them? Study the hexagons highlighted in figure 2-43 and try to detect their special properties.

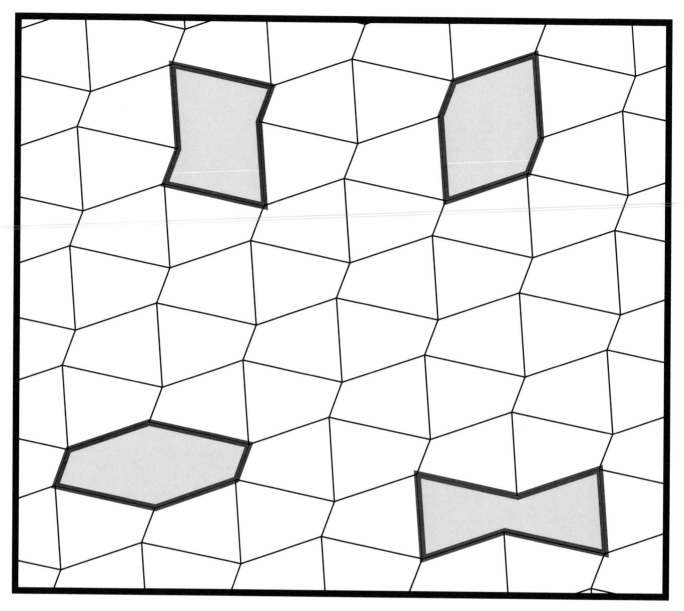

Fig. 2-43. Pairs of tessellating quadrilaterals form special hexagons that also tessellate.

You should have observed that each of these special hexagons displays two properties:

1. Opposite sides are congruent.

2. Opposite sides are parallel.

As you can see, a quadrilateral tessellation can introduce as many as four new tessellating special hexagons. Tessellations of the four hexagonal shapes shown in figure 2-43 are illustrated in figure 2-44. Each pattern in figure 2-44 is formed by congruent pairs of the same quadrilateral, arranged in different positions.

Fig. 2-44. Tessellating special hexagons formed by two congruent quadrilaterals

If we could continue our investigation of which general polygons will tessellate the plane, we would find that in general, only triangles and quadrilaterals *always* tessellate by themselves. We have seen examples of some pentagons and special hexagons that tessellate, too. Other polygons or combinations of polygons will sometimes tessellate, under certain conditions. Figures 2-45 through 2-50 show tessellations of polygons with seven, eight, nine, ten, twelve, and eighteen sides; however, in none of these cases will *all* forms of that polygon tessellate. Now we may ask: Which *regular* polygons tessellate? This question we will explore in the next chapter.

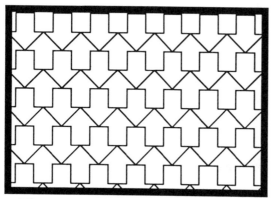

Fig. 2-45. Tessellating heptagons

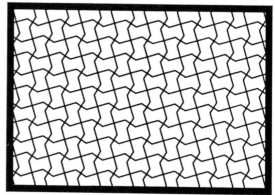

Fig. 2-46. Tessellating octagons

Fig. 2-47. Tessellating nonagons

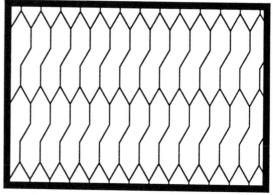

Fig. 2-48. Tessellating decagons

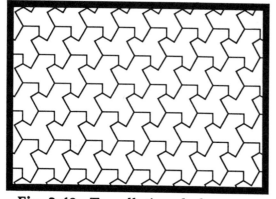

Fig. 2-49. Tessellating dodecagons

Fig. 2-50. Tessellating 18-gons

Chapter 3

TESSELLATING POLYGONS

(Specific)

In chapter 2 we explored which general polygons would tessellate the plane. We concluded that only two types of polygonal shapes will *always* tessellate: triangles and quadrilaterals. In this chapter, we will explore which *regular* polygons tessellate by themselves. In addition, we will investigate which combinations of two or more regular polygons tessellate the plane. Recall that a regular polygon is one with all its angles and sides congruent. Examples of eight regular polygons (triangle through decagon) are illustrated in figure 3-1. Observe that as the number of sides in the regular polygon increases, the closer it comes to appearing like a circle. In fact, it would be difficult to differentiate a regular 100-gon from a circle.

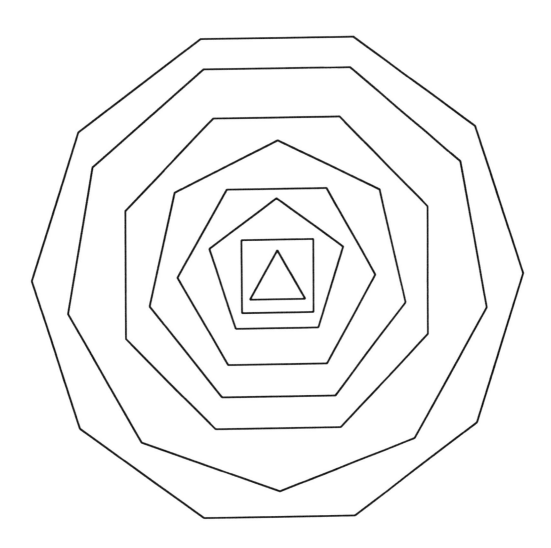

Fig. 3-1. Eight regular polygons

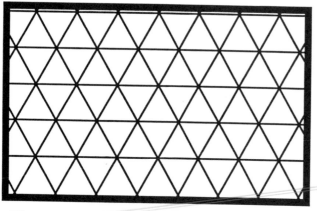

Fig. 3-2. Tessellating equilateral triangles

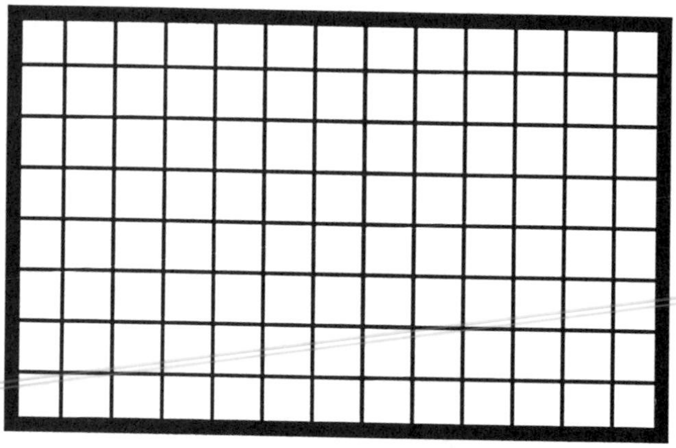

Fig. 3-3. Tessellating squares

Since we already know that every triangle tessellates and every quadrilateral tessellates, we know that their special regular forms will tessellate. Examples of these regular tessellations are shown in figures 3-2 and 3-3. We are quite familiar with tessellations of squares and equilateral triangles in patterns that we see around us daily in design and decoration.

In the preceding chapter, we learned that hexagons with opposite sides that are both parallel and congruent (hexagons made from two congruent quadrilaterals) will tessellate. In figure 3-4, we can observe that the opposite sides of a regular hexagon appear to be parallel; they always are. Further, we know that the opposite sides are congruent, since all six sides are congruent. We should, therefore, expect this special shape to tessellate the plane; figure 3-5 shows that it does. Like the previous two regular tessellations, this one is quite familiar to us. We have seen regular hexagon tessellations in numerous places, including kitchen and bathroom tile, quilt designs, honeycombs, and chicken wire.

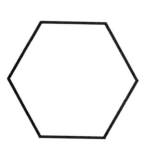

Fig. 3-4.
A regular hexagon

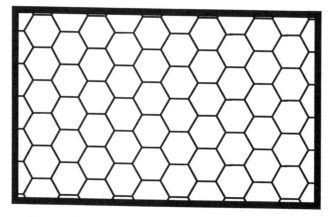

Fig. 3-5. Tessellating regular hexagons

We have seen that regular triangles, squares, and hexagons all tessellate by themselves; but what about the regular pentagon? Figure 3-6 shows three congruent regular pentagons positioned in the plane so that they share a common vertex. Notice that three pentagons so arranged do not form a perigon (360° angle); there is a slight gap. From this we could speculate that each congruent angle of the regular pentagon contains slightly less than 120° (one-third of a perigon). If we place a fourth regular pentagon at the common vertex, the four shapes do not tessellate; they overlap (figure 3-7).

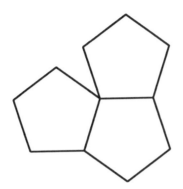 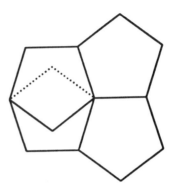

Fig. 3-6. Three regular pentagons   **Fig. 3-7.** Four regular pentagons

Dividing a pentagon by drawing two of its diagonals demonstrates that any pentagon can be divided into three triangles. This means that the sum of the angles of any pentagon is always $3 \times 180°$ or 540°. Dividing 540° by the five angles, we see that each angle in a regular pentagon will measure exactly 108° (figure 3-8). Because 108° does not divide 360° exactly, we can conclude that regular pentagons will not tessellate by themselves. Figure 3-9 shows an attempt to tessellate with regular pentagons.

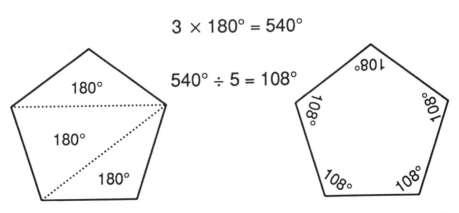

Fig. 3-8. The sum of the interior angles of a pentagon is 540°.

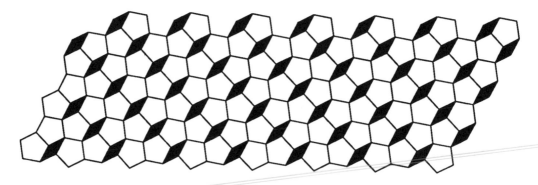

Fig. 3-9. Regular pentagons leave parallelogram gaps, forming a two-shape tessellation.

It seems that we can generalize as follows:

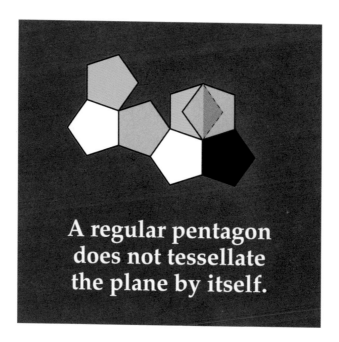

A regular pentagon does not tessellate the plane by itself.

Dividing polygons into triangles to determine the sum of their interior angles, as we just did with the pentagon, provides a strategy for determining which other regular polygons, if any, tessellate by themselves. We can divide any regular polygon into triangles. Knowing that the sum of the angles of a triangle equals 180°, we multiply 180° times the number of triangles that we formed; this gives us the sum of all the angles in the polygon. If we divide this total by the number of congruent angles in the regular polygon, we arrive at the measure of each of angle. Figures 3-10 through 3-12 show how we determine the measures of the angles of regular hexagons, heptagons, and octagons, which in turn enables us to learn whether or not these shapes tessellate.

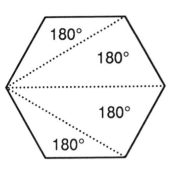

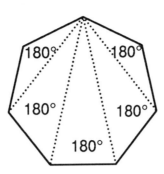

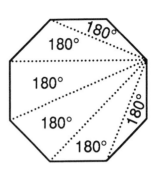

$$4 \times 180° = 720°$$
$$720° \div 6 = 120°$$

Fig. 3-10.
A hexagon divides
into four triangles.

$$5 \times 180° = 900°$$
$$900° \div 7 = 128\ 4/7°$$

Fig. 3-11.
A heptagon divides
into five triangles.

$$6 \times 180° = 1080°$$
$$1080° \div 8 = 135°$$

Fig. 3-12.
An octagon divides
into six triangles.

As you can see in figure 3-13, the three 120° angles of the regular hexagons exactly fill all the space around a common vertex point. Just figuring the angle measures tells us this, because 120° divides 360° exactly. Thus three hexagons will fit around a vertex point with no gaps or overlapping; regular hexagons tessellate. The angle measures of the regular seven- and eight-sided polygons, however, do not exactly divide 360°; therefore they do not fill the space around a common vertex without overlapping (figures 3-14 and 3-15). We conclude that regular heptagons and octagons will not tessellate.

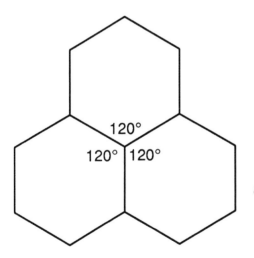

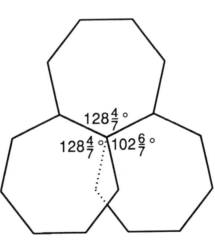

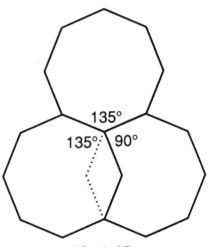

Fig. 3-13.
Regular hexagons
tessellate.

Fig. 3-14.
Regular heptagons
do not tessellate.

Fig. 3-15.
Regular octagons
do not tessellate.

Let's see what generalizations we could make here. As the polygons increase in number of sides, the size of their angles also increases. When hexagons fill the space around a point, three equal angles meet at a common vertex point. Since the polygon angles get larger as the number of sides increases, the next time we could fill 360° with equal angles would be when we had two angles measuring 180°. It is impossible to have a regular polygon each of whose angles measure 180° (since that is a straight line); therefore we cannot have regular polygons with more than six sides that tessellate the plane. Our conclusion is as follows:

There are only three regular tessellations.

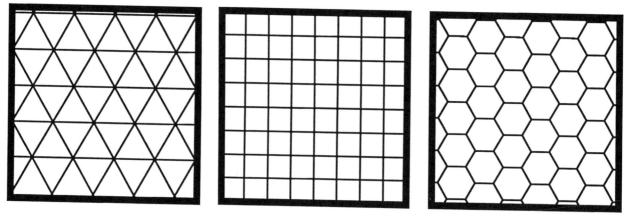

Fig. 3-16. The three regular tessellations

Tessellations of Two or More Regular Polygons

We have seen the importance of the angle measure of polygons in determining whether or not a given polygon will tessellate. In this section we will explore which *combinations* of regular polygons tessellate.

Remember, we have learned how to find the angle measure of regular polygons quite simply by drawing diagonals to divide them into triangles. Knowing the angle measure of certain regular polygons enables us to determine which combinations total 360° and thus exactly fill the space around a vertex point. Figure 3-17 lists the key regular polygons and their angle measures. Using the general formula for an *n*-gon, we can find the angle measure of any regular polygon.

POLYGON	NUMBER OF SIDES/ANGLES	SUM OF INTERIOR ANGLES	MEASURE OF EACH INTERIOR ANGLE (REGULAR POLYGONS)
triangle	3	180°	60°
quadrilateral	4	360°	90°
pentagon	5	540°	108°
hexagon	6	720°	120°
heptagon	7	900°	$128\frac{4}{7}°$
octagon	8	1080°	135°
nonagon	9	1260°	140°
decagon	10	1440°	144°
dodecagon	12	1800°	150°
15-gon	15	2340°	156°
18-gon	18	2880°	160°
20-gon	20	3240°	162°
24-gon	24	3960°	165°
42-gon	42	7200°	$171\frac{3}{7}°$
.	.	.	.
.	.	.	.
.	.	.	.
n-gon	n	$(n-2)\,180°$	$\dfrac{(n-2)\,180°}{n}$

Fig. 3-17. Interior angle measures in selected regular polygons

The general problem of filling the space around a point with regular polygons was first solved in 1785 by The Rev. Mr. Jones. Jones listed the following limitations regarding the number and kinds of polygons that can be fitted together around a single point:

1. There cannot be more than six polygons, because six angles of equilateral triangles are equal to four right angles.
2. There cannot be less than three polygons, because an angle of any regular polygon is less than two right angles.
3. There cannot be more than three "sorts" of polygons used at once, because the three "sorts" whose angles are smallest are the equilateral triangle, the square, and the regular pentagon. The sum of these three angles, 60° + 90° + 108°, is 258°. For four different regular polygons the smallest possible sum is 60° + 90° + 108° + 120°, which is 378°.
4. If there are four polygons, two must be of the same "sort."
5. If there are five polygons, there are two possibilities:
   (a) Two of each of two "sorts" and one of another;
   (b) Three of one "sort" and one each of two other "sorts."*

*From Bradley, A. D., *The Geometry of Repeating Design and Geometry of Design for High Schools.* New York: Teachers College, Columbia University, 1933.

Using Jones's logic, we can find what possible combinations of regular polygons will fill all the space around a point. Here's where our chart of angle sizes (figure 3-17) is very helpful. Kepler first addressed the problem of finding tessellating angle combinations nearly 400 years ago; mathematicians have now determined that 21 arrangements of regular polygons will fill the space around a point, as shown in figure 3-18. (Although the language of Jones's fifth limitation seems technically inconsistent with combinations 3.3.3.4.4 and 3.3.3.3.6, he apparently did not mean to exclude them.) Note that there are only 17 different angle combinations; the additional four arrangements are made by placing some of the same combinations of polygons in a different order.

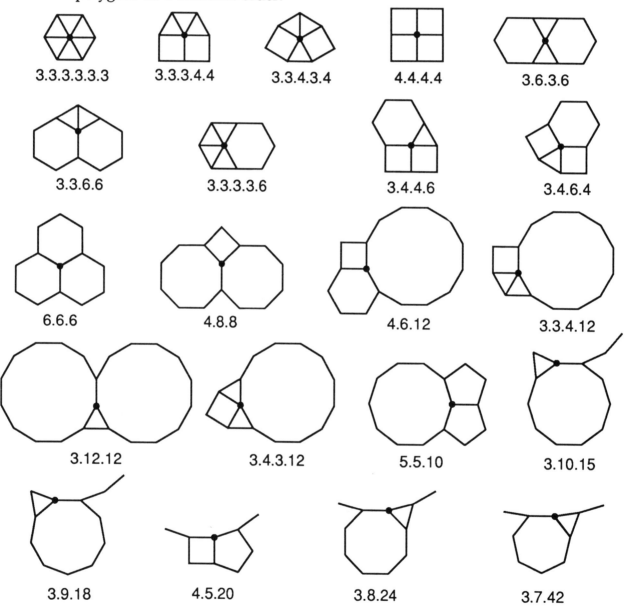

Fig. 3-18. The 21 arrangements of regular polygon combinations that fill the space around a point

In the numerical notation that we use to identify each arrangement, we list the polygon sides (angles) starting with a given vertex and proceeding sequentially around the point. Figure 3-19 shows an example of a combination that appears twice but in a different order, creating a quite different pattern.

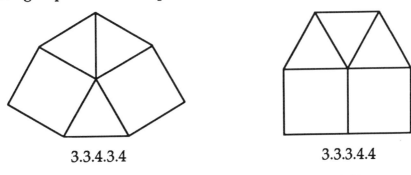

3.3.4.3.4   3.3.3.4.4

Fig. 3-19. The same polygon combinations in different order

Readers who are teaching secondary mathematics or those with a strong math background may be interested in the algebraic analysis of all possible arrangements of regular polygons that fill space around a point. This information can be found in the appendix, page 245.

Now that we have identified the 21 arrangements of regular polygons that fill the space around a point, let's investigate which of these will tessellate the plane. Filling all the space about a point guaranteed a tessellation when we were using congruent regular polygons, but it is no guarantee when we are using more than one shape. We need to look carefully at each combination to see if we can continue to build a pattern that will be infinite. In figure 3-20, arrangement 3.3.4.3.4 has been extended and appears to tessellate. Observe that at every vertex point in the tessellation, we find the identical set of polygons *in the same order.*

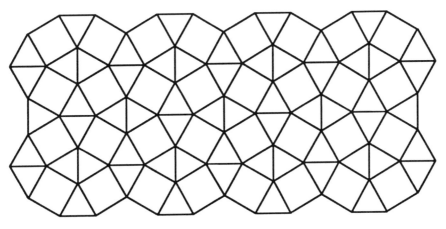

Fig. 3-20. A tessellation of squares and equilateral triangles

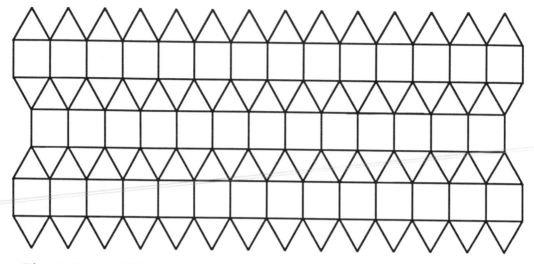

Fig. 3-21. A different tessellation of squares and equilateral triangles

Extending the other combination of three triangles and two squares (3.3.3.4.4) shown in figure 3-19 also forms a tessellation, but in a much different pattern. Again, though, at each vertex point in figure 3-21 we find the same set of polygons in the same sequence.

We call the patterns that have been formed in figures 3-20 and 3-21 *semiregular* tessellations. A semiregular tessellation has two properties:

1. It is formed by regular polygons.

2. The arrangement of polygons at every vertex point is identical.

If you like to discover things on your own, you might like to stop reading here momentarily and see if you can discover all the possible semiregular tessellations by yourself. Armed with information about angle measures (figure 3-17) and the 21 regular polygon arrangements shown in figure 3-18, you should be able to discover most of the semiregular tessellations without much difficulty. Here is a clue to get you started:

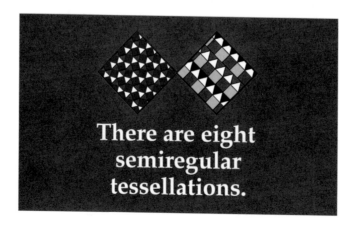

There are eight
semiregular
tessellations.

The eight semiregular and three regular tessellations are sometimes called *Archimedean, homogeneous,* or *uniform tilings.* In semiregular tessellations, *all* the vertex points are formed by identical combinations of regular polygons, as you can see by studying the designs in figure 3-23. The tessellation in figure 3-22 is made from regular polygons, and it does form a pattern that can be extended indefinitely. Nonetheless, it is *not* semiregular because there are two different vertex points with different combinations of polygons (3.4.6.4 and 3.3.4.3.4, as highlighted in the figure).

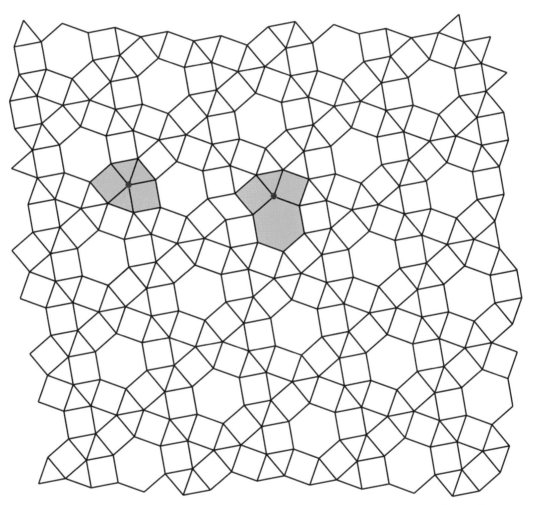

Fig. 3-22. A tessellation of regular polygons that is not semiregular

Further examples of tessellating regular polygons that are *not* semiregular tessellations are shown in figure 3-24. There are an infinite number of these patterns that do not have the same combination of angles at every vertex point. These types of tessellations, along with many others that are not discussed in this book, are explained in rigorous detail by Grünbaum and Shephard in *Tilings and Patterns.*

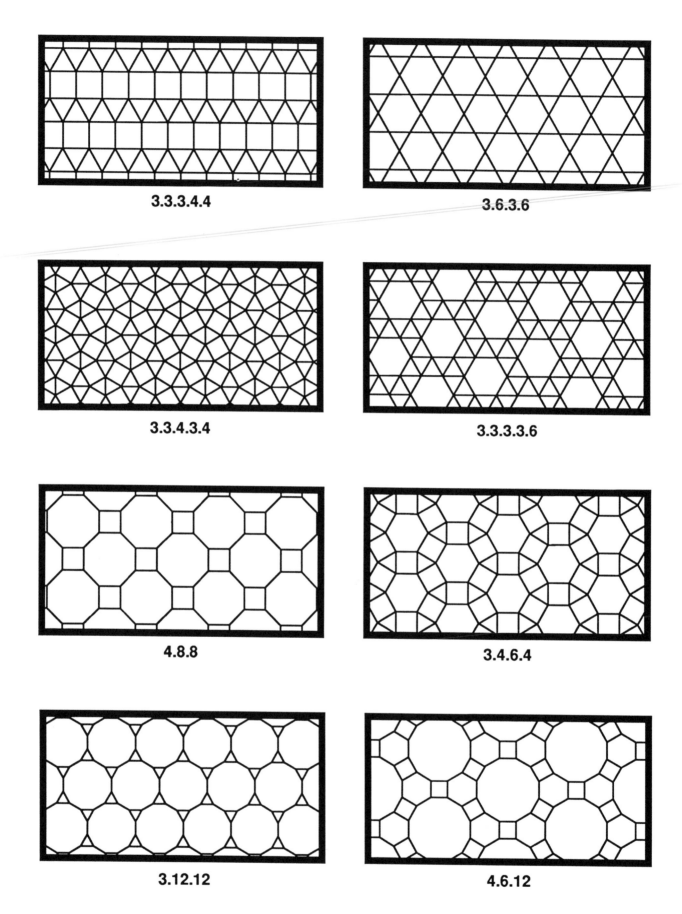

Fig. 3-23. The eight semiregular tessellations

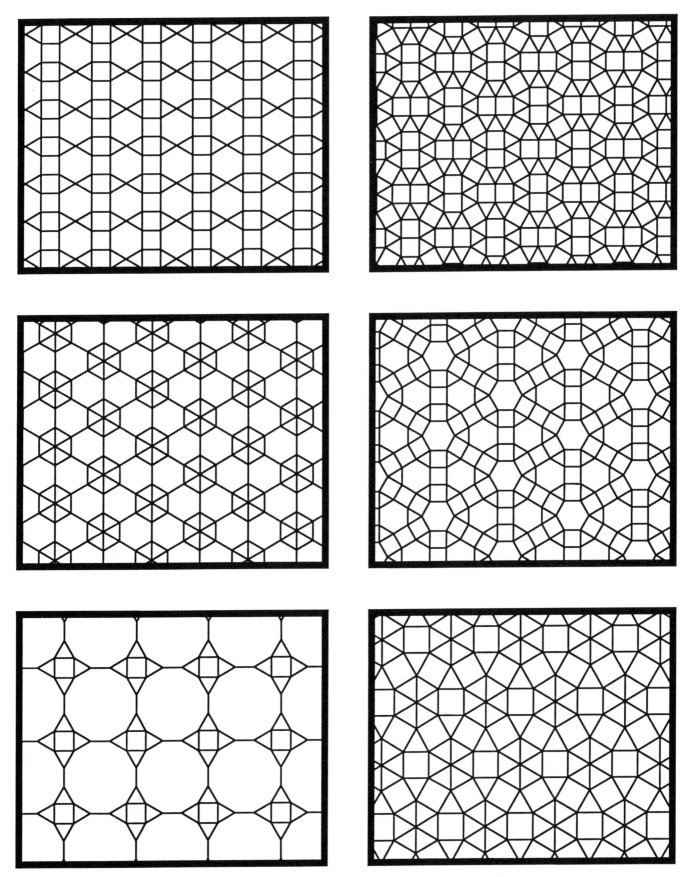

Fig. 3-24. Tessellations of regular polygons that contain more than one type of vertex point

Before we leave our exploration of the tessellation of regular polygons, let's look at another variation. All the examples we have considered thus far have been created with polygons that share common edges and vertices. That is, all shared edges coincide. It is possible to tessellate the plane with regular polygons that are not arranged in edge-to-edge patterns. Four such patterns are shown in figure 3-25, and an additional two are shown in figure 3-26. In general, we are less interested in tessellations of this type as they appear much less frequently in design applications.

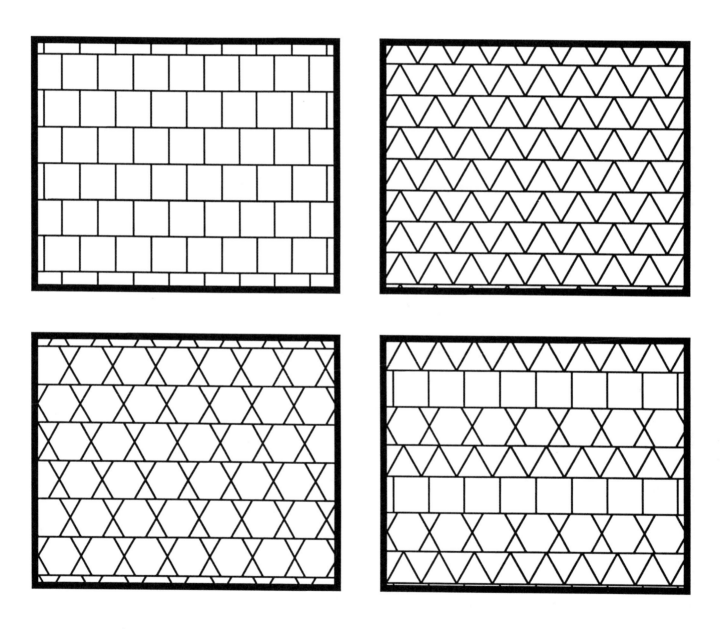

Fig. 3-25. Tessellations of regular polygons not positioned edge-to-edge

Fig. 3-26. Tessellating non-congruent regular polygons

We have now completed our investigation of which regular polygons will tessellate, both by themselves and in combinations. In the next chapter we will explore another important property of tessellations: their symmetries.

Chapter 4

SYMMETRY & TRANSFORMATIONS

Most of us know the word *symmetry* as used by artists, architects, and scientists to refer to the balance of form or harmonious arrangements in a painting, a sculpture, a building, or in natural phenomena such as crystals or plant and animal forms. Symmetry also happens to be a property of all tessellations. We look for symmetries as we explore these designs; locating the symmetries in a particular tessellation helps us identify its underlying grid pattern.

We will discuss several different types of symmetry in this chapter. Take a look at the four designs in figure 4-1. All are symmetrical, but each has a quite different kind of symmetry. To understand the differences, we will look at how each design might have been created by certain special movements of a part of the figure—movements that mathematicians call *transformations*.

Fig. 4-1. Designs exhibiting four different types of symmetry

Mathematicians recognize different types of transformations, but in this book we are concerned only with *rigid* transformations, which move figures without changing their size or shape. A transformation can be thought of as a motion that moves a figure from one location on a plane to a new location on that same plane. Recognizing these transformations helps us analyze and create tessellations. In this book we will use four types of transformation: (1) translation, (2) rotation, (3) reflection, and (4) glide reflection. Let's explore the differences among them.

In figure 4-2, the two-color arrow on the left is moved to a new location by sliding it down and to the right. In the process, every point on the first arrow is moved the same distance in the same direction. Such a motion is the transformation that we call a *translation* or a *slide*.

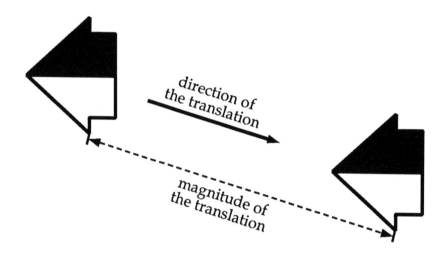

Fig. 4-2. A translation or a slide

The smaller arrow indicates the *direction* of the translation. The distance between any two corresponding points on the original and the translated shape is called the *magnitude* (or size) of the translation. The dashed arrow in figure 4-2 shows the magnitude of this particular translation. Note that the orientation of a figure does *not* change when it undergoes a translation.

When we move a figure to a new location on a plane by rotating it about a fixed point, we call this transformation a *rotation* or a *turn*. Figure 4-3 demonstrates this motion.

To better understand a rotation, you can recreate it using figure 4-4 and tracing paper or acetate. Trace the two-color arrow on the upper left, then lay your tracing precisely over the figure. Anchor the tracing paper (or acetate) to the plane of this page by pressing a sharp pencil onto the marked point. By rotating the tracing paper through an appropriate angle about that point, you can make your tracing coincide exactly with the arrow in its new location and orientation at the lower right.

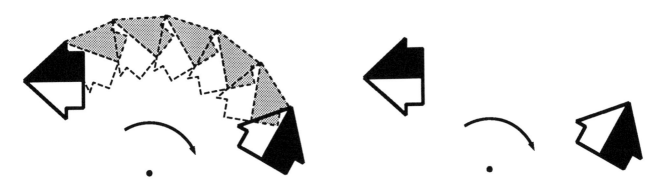

Fig. 4-3. A rotation or a turn   Fig. 4-4. Diagram for exploring a rotation

The point in the plane about which a shape is rotated is called the *center of rotation*. Lines connecting the center of rotation with corresponding points on the original shape and the rotated shape form the *angle of rotation*. The size of this angle gives us the magnitude of the rotation.

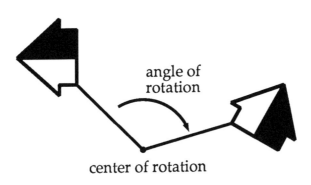

angle of
rotation

center of rotation

Fig. 4-5. The center of rotation and the angle of rotation

We can think of a rotation as the motion of a windshield wiper sweeping across a car's windshield. The point about which the wiper turns is the center of rotation; the size of a single sweep gives the magnitude of the angle of rotation.

In the third type of transformation, we move a figure to a new location on a plane by flipping it about a line in that plane. We call this motion a *reflection* or a *flip*. The line about which the figure moves is the *line of reflection*. This transformation is illustrated in figure 4-6 with the same two-color arrows that we earlier translated and rotated.

If we placed a mirror along the line of reflection, in a plane perpendicular to the plane of this page (figure 4-7), then the "mirror image" of the original figure would coincide with the figure in its new location. The use of the word *reflection* to name this transformation emphasizes this mirror-image relationship.

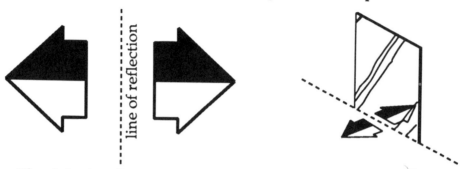

Fig. 4-6. A reflection or a flip

Fig. 4-7. The line of reflection suggests a mirror image.

In the final type of transformation, we combine the motions of reflection and translation to move a figure to its new location—first by flipping it about a line of reflection, then by sliding it along a straight line parallel to that line of reflection. Such a motion, illustrated in figure 4-8, is called a *glide reflection*. We could, of course, perform the steps in the other order, sliding the figure first and then reflecting it; the result is the same in either case.

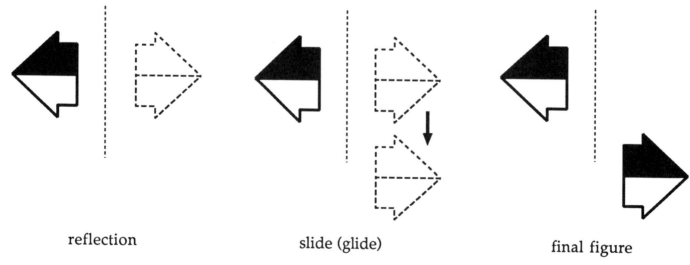

reflection   slide (glide)   final figure

Fig. 4-8. A glide reflection

Note that to achieve a glide reflection, neither a translation alone nor a reflection alone will give us the desired effect. Hence, in this case, we regard neither the translation nor the reflection by itself as a transformation; instead they are seen together as the steps of a single transformation.

It is interesting to compare a glide reflection with a 180° rotation. In figures 4-9 and 4-10, what difference (if any) do you see in the two transformations? If the arrow had not been half dark and half light, would the two different transformations have produced essentially the same result?

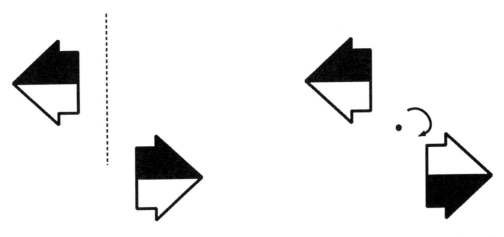

Fig. 4-9. A glide reflection   Fig. 4-10. A rotation of 180°

Now that we have identified four types of transformation, let's see how these operations help us create the four different types of symmetry: translational symmetry, rotational symmetry, reflective symmetry, and glide-reflection symmetry.

Translational Symmetry

Suppose the pattern in figure 4-11 extends infinitely to the left and to the right. It can then be made to coincide with itself by sliding or translating it to the left or to the right. If you were to trace the pattern onto a sheet of tracing paper or acetate, you could verify this for yourself.

Fig. 4-11. A design with translational symmetry

Such a design is said to have *translational symmetry*. When a figure has been translated onto itself exactly, we say it is *in coincidence*. The shortest translation that results in coincidence is the translation between any two adjacent corresponding points, as illustrated by the dashed lines in figure 4-12. We call this distance the *magnitude* of the translation.

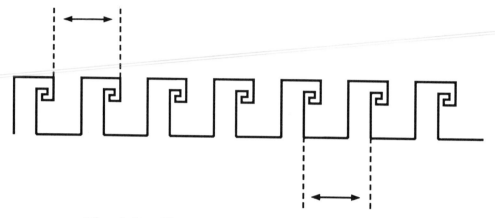

Fig. 4-12. The magnitude of the translation

In general, then, a figure has *translational symmetry* if it coincides with itself after an appropriate translation. Every point in the figure moves the same distance in the same direction. The shortest distance that results in coincidence in a given direction is the *magnitude* of the translation in that direction.

Let's see how this works in a tessellation, like the tessellation of congruent scalene quadrilaterals shown in figure 4-13. This tessellation has translational symmetry. Note that all the red quadrilaterals

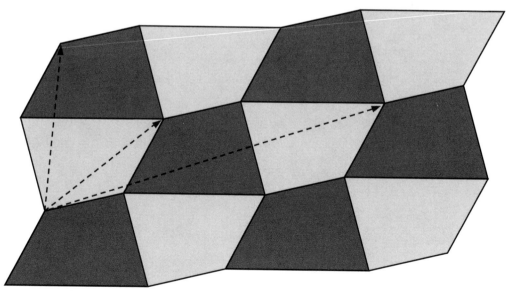

Fig. 4-13. A tessellation with translational symmetry

have precisely the same orientation. We can make the tessellation coincide with itself by sliding it until any quadrilateral of one color coincides exactly with another quadrilateral of that same color. The arrows show three possible directions for this translation.

Since there are infinitely many identically oriented quadrilaterals, there are infinitely many different possibilities for the direction of the translation. This fact is valid for *all* tessellations, whatever their type of tessellating regions, and whatever other kinds of symmetry they possess.

Rotational Symmetry

Now let's consider the design shown in figure 4-14. Suppose that you trace the figure, lay your tracing precisely over the original figure, press with a sharp pencil on the marked point, then rotate the tracing paper about this point until the tracing and the original figure again coincide. This will happen in less than one full turn. Such a figure is said to have *rotational symmetry*. The marked point is called the *center of rotation*.

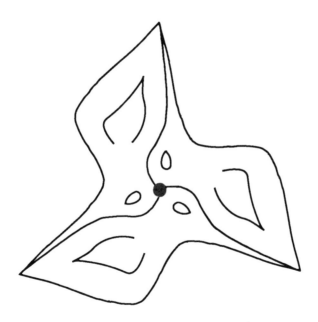

Fig. 4-14. A design with rotational symmetry

You could use your tracing to verify that the traced figure will coincide with the original figure exactly three times in one full turn, as shown in figure 4-15. Because of this property, we can say that the figure has *three-fold* (3-fold) rotational symmetry.

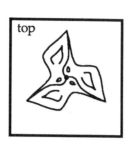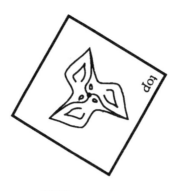

initial position   120° rotation   240° rotation

Fig. 4-15. A figure with three-fold symmetry, shown in the three positions in which it coincides with itself

For this particular figure, the size of the angle between successive fits is 120°, or 360°/3. We call this the *angle of rotation*.

In general, then, a figure has *rotational symmetry* if it coincides with itself after an appropriate rotation of less than one full turn. The point about which all other points in the figure move is called the *center of rotation*. We say that a figure has *n-fold* rotational symmetry if it coincides with itself exactly *n* times in one full turn. The smallest angle that results in coincidence, or the *angle of rotation*, is given by the formula 360°/*n*. Figures 4-16 through 4-19 present further examples of figures with rotational symmetry.

Fig. 4-16. Two-fold rotation; angle of rotation: 180°

Fig. 4-17. Three-fold rotation; angle of rotation: 120°

Fig. 4-18. Five-fold rotation; angle of rotation: 72°

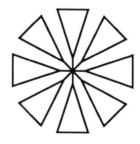

Fig. 4-19. Eight-fold rotation; angle of rotation: 45°

All *regular* polygons have rotational symmetry. The center of rotation is the center of the polygon. A regular polygon with n sides has n-fold rotational symmetry; this is readily verified by observing the polygons in figure 4-20.

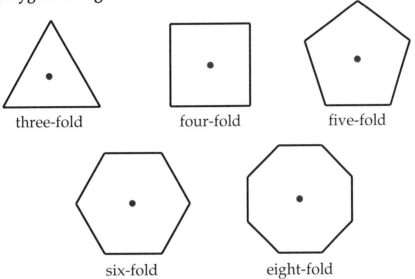

three-fold   four-fold   five-fold

six-fold   eight-fold

Fig. 4-20. Regular polygons have rotational symmetry.

All three regular tessellations have rotational symmetry. Consider, for example, the tessellation of equilateral triangles illustrated in figure 4-21. The center of each triangle is a center of three-fold rotation; each vertex of each triangle is a center of six-fold rotation; and the midpoint of each side of each triangle is a center of two-fold rotation.

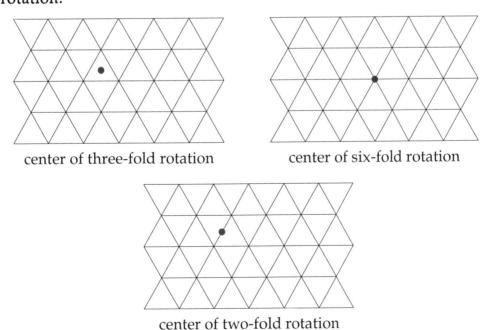

center of three-fold rotation   center of six-fold rotation

center of two-fold rotation

Fig. 4-21. A triangle tessellation has rotational symmetry.

The rotational symmetries for all three regular tessellations are shown in figure 4-22. If you are having trouble visualizing the symmetries, try tracing the figures and rotating your tracings as described earlier.

Note that the centers of all polygons in a given tessellation are interchangeable or *equivalent*, as are all the vertices and all the midpoints of the sides. Each tessellation has exactly three different (*non-equivalent*) centers of rotation.

Fig. 4-22. The rotational symmetries of the three regular tessellations

equilateral triangle
three-fold at the centers
six-fold at the vertices
two-fold at the midpoints
of the sides

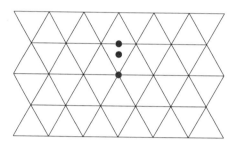

square
four-fold at the centers
four-fold at the vertices
two-fold at the midpoints
of the sides

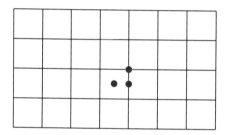

regular hexagon
six-fold at the centers
three-fold at the vertices
two-fold at the midpoints
of the sides

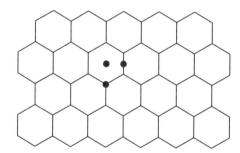

The semiregular tessellations also display rotational symmetries, but there is no simple pattern. For practice in identifying symmetries in tessellations, let's look at the semiregular tessellations. In figures 4-23 through 4-26, we identify some points of symmetry with red dots. Determine whether the marked point is a center of rotation, and if so, what the symmetry of the rotation is (i.e., two-fold, three-fold, six-fold). If the point is *not* a center of rotation, locate some other points on the tessellation to which the marked point could translate. If you can't do this by visualizing, trace the patterns and explore them that way.

Then, in the next four semiregular tessellations (figures 4-27 through 4-30), see if you can identify all the different centers of rotation and the symmetries (i.e., two-fold) of each. (See page 84 for answers.)

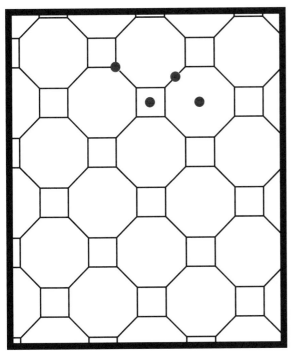

Fig. 4-23. Tessellation 4.8.8

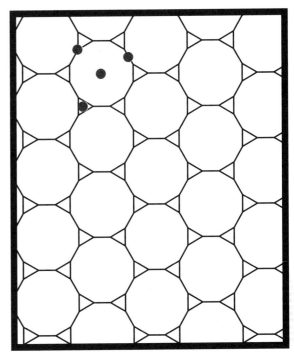

Fig. 4-24. Tessellation 3.12.12

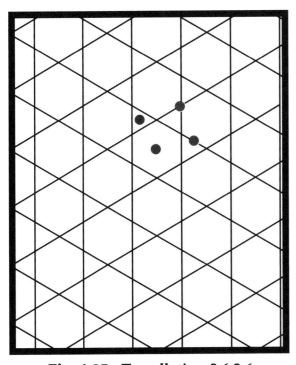

Fig. 4-25. Tessellation 3.6.3.6

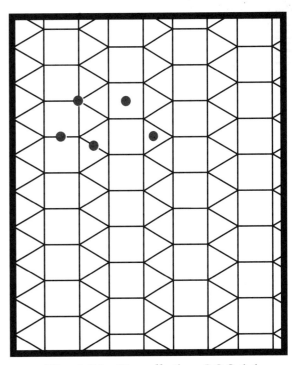

Fig. 4-26. Tessellation 3.3.3.4.4

Fig. 4-27. Tessellation 4.6.12

Fig. 4-28. Tessellation 3.4.6.4

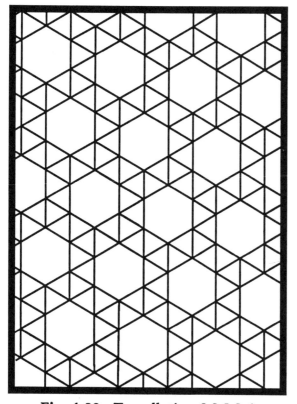

Fig. 4-29. Tessellation 3.3.3.3.6

Fig. 4-30. Tessellation 3.3.4.3.4

When we look for symmetries in the tessellations of *irregular* polygons, we find several interesting results. Parallelograms taken alone have two-fold rotational symmetry about their centers. Tessellations of parallelograms have two-fold rotational symmetry about the center, the vertices, and the midpoints of the sides of each parallelogram (figure 4-31).

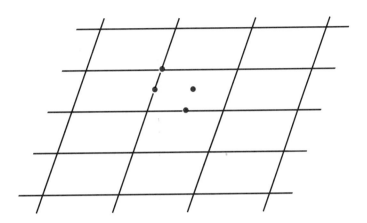

Fig. 4-31. Centers of rotational symmetry for tessellating parallelograms

Tessellations of scalene quadrilaterals have two-fold rotational symmetry about the midpoints of the sides of each quadrilateral. Thus there are four different centers of two-fold rotation, marked with red dots in figure 4-32. Similarly, tessellations of scalene triangles have three different centers of two-fold rotation.

Although we could further explore rotational symmetry and tessellations, this is all we really need for the purposes of this book.

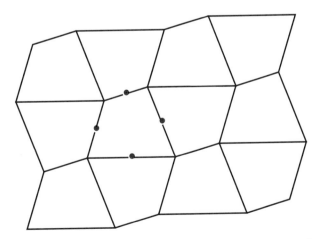

Fig. 4-32. Centers of rotational symmetry for tessellating quadrilaterals

Next we will investigate reflective symmetry, an example of which appears in figure 4-33. If you were to trace the clown face and fold your tracing along the vertical dashed line, you will find that one half fits exactly over the other half. In other words, if the original illustration could be flipped about the vertical dashed line, left side to right side and right side to left, it would coincide with itself.

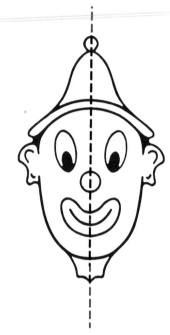

Fig. 4-33. Illustration with
reflective symmetry

If you were to place a mirror along the vertical line, in a plane perpendicular to the plane of this page, you would find that the mirror image of one half of the clown face is exactly the same as the other half of the original face, lying behind the mirror. The two halves of the figure are mirror images of each other. Thus we say that the figure has *reflective symmetry*, and the vertical line is its *line of reflection*. This type of symmetry is what the word brings to mind for many people; asked to name a symmetrical figure, many of us would name a heart, a Christmas tree, a butterfly, or other such examples of reflective symmetry.

In general, then, a figure has *reflective symmetry* if it coincides with itself after reflection about an appropriate line, or a *line of reflection*. A line of reflection divides a figure into two congruent parts. In other words, it bisects a figure.

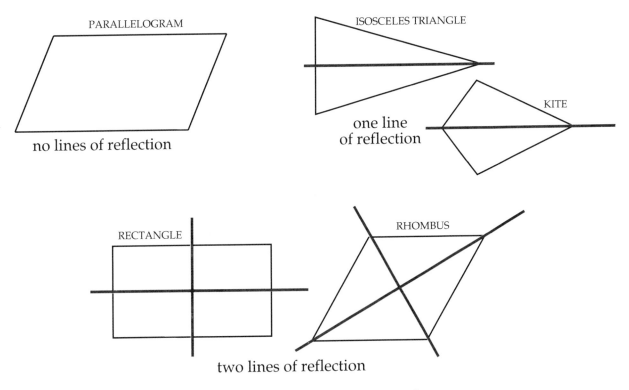

Fig. 4-34. Lines of reflection in various polygons

A figure can have one or more lines of reflection. The number of lines of reflection in a polygon is an important property of that polygon. A polygon may have *no* lines of reflection or it may have several, as illustrated in figures 4-34 and 4-35. Parallelograms, other than rectangles and rhombi, have no lines of reflection. Isosceles triangles other than equilateral, and kite-shaped quadrilaterals other than rhombi, have a single line of reflection. Rectangles and rhombi, other than squares, have exactly two lines of reflection. *Regular* polygons with *n* sides have exactly *n* lines of reflection.

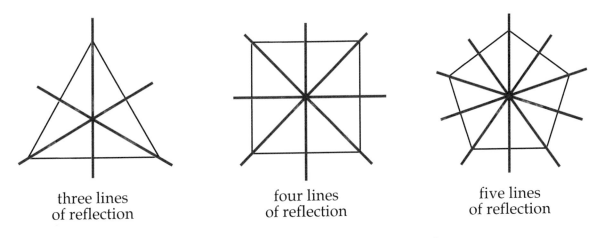

Fig. 4-35. Lines of reflection in regular polygons

Figure 4-36 shows a number of patterns extracted from tessellations. Try to visualize the centers of rotation and the lines of symmetry of each pattern. Which patterns have both rotational and reflective symmetry? (See page 85 for answers.)

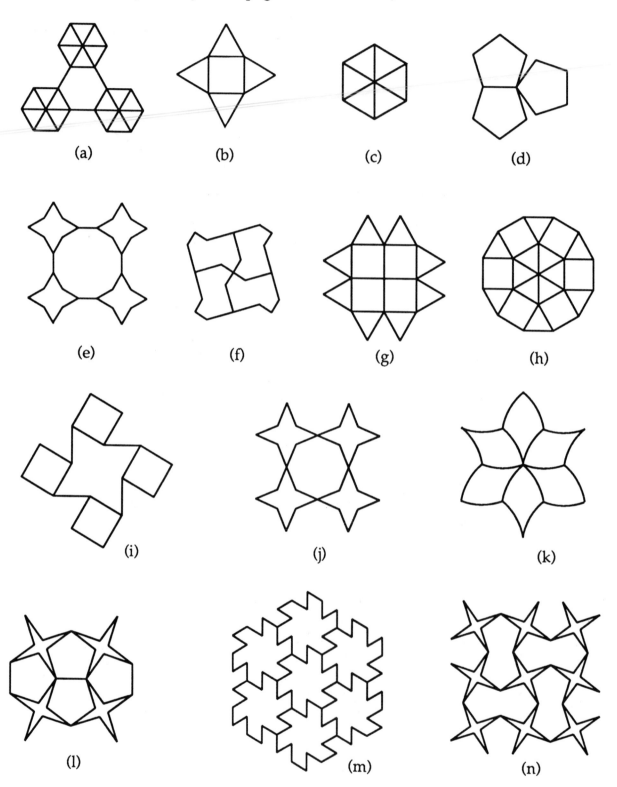

(a)   (b)   (c)   (d)

(e)   (f)   (g)   (h)

(i)   (j)   (k)

(l)   (m)   (n)

Fig. 4-36. Symmetrical polygonal patterns

All polygonal tessellations with reflective symmetry have lines of reflection that are coincident with the lines of reflection for the individual polygons in the design. In many cases, the tessellation has additional lines of reflection that are coincident with the *sides* of the individual polygons. This is true in the three regular tessellations. Lines of reflection run from the vertices through the centers of the polygons, and lines coincident with the sides of the polygons are also lines of reflection.

When we superimpose *all* lines of symmetry on a regular tessellation, the cumulative effect can be overwhelming. Consider, for example, the tessellation of regular hexagons. A closeup of a *single* hexagon within that tessellation, with portions of its immediate neighbors, is shown in figure 4-37. The lines of reflection are represented by dashed red lines.

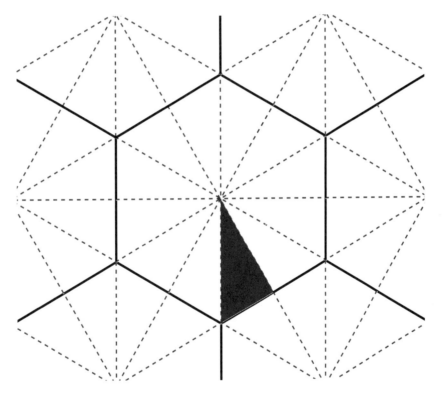

Fig. 4-37. Lines of symmetry in a tessellation of regular hexagons

The implications of this figure are amazing. Suppose you were to place a tiny mirror on each of the three sides of the shaded triangle, each in a plane perpendicular to the plane of this page and each just meeting its two companion mirrors at the vertices of said triangle. A tiny insect sitting on the shaded triangle and looking into any of the three mirrors would see the *entire* tessellation extending to infinity—accompanied by infinitely many images of the insect itself!

We have already seen that a figure can have more than one kind of symmetry. Regular polygons, for example, have both rotational and reflective symmetry. But what about a pattern like the one in figure 4-38? Suppose this pattern extends infinitely to the left and to the right. It then has translational symmetry, a fact that we can easily visualize (or, if needed, verify with a tracing). But we can also look at this pattern another way, as demonstrated in figure 4-39.

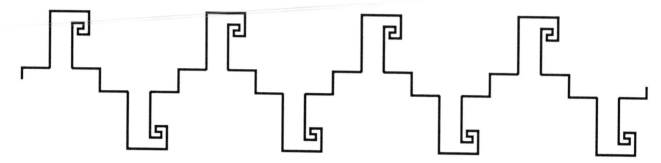

Fig. 4-38. Figure with translational symmetry

Suppose that we first reflect the figure about the dashed horizontal line, then translate it horizontally. This sequence of motions will bring it into coincidence. Because of this, we say that the pattern has glide-reflection symmetry.

Fig. 4-39. Visualize a translation, then a reflection of the first element.

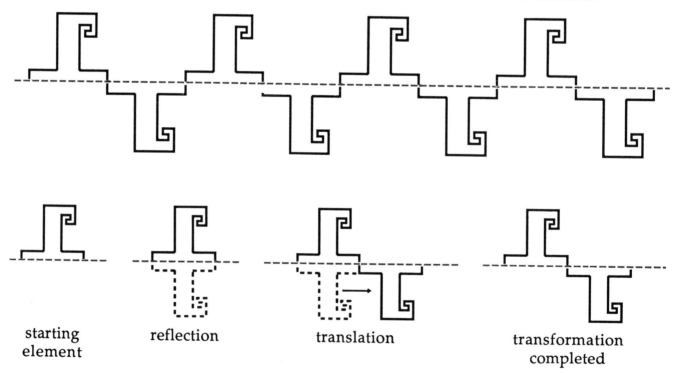

starting
element

reflection

translation

transformation
completed

Note that reflection *alone* does not result in coincidence; the reflection *must* be followed by a translation in a direction parallel to the line of reflection.

We say, then, that a figure has *glide-reflection symmetry* if it coincides with itself after reflection about a given line followed by translation in a direction parallel to that line.

The nature of glide reflection produces an interesting result, as demonstrated in figures 4-40 and 4-41. This design has translational symmetry, a fact that is easy to visualize. It also has reflective symmetry; the dashed horizontal line in figure 4-41 is the line of reflection. If we apply the definition literally, we must conclude that this pattern also has glide-reflection symmetry. Indeed, *any* figure with both translational and reflective symmetry will automatically have glide-reflection symmetry.

Fig. 4-40. Visualize the translational symmetry.

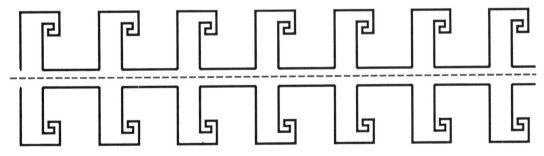

Fig. 4-41. Now visualize the reflective symmetry.

The inverse of this statement is not necessarily true, as our previous example (figure 4-38) illustrates. Like that pattern, a figure can have glide-reflection symmetry without having reflective symmetry. Figures 4-42 through 4-46 should clarify this very important point.

The trail left on a sandy beach by a biped hopping on one foot has translational symmetry alone.

Fig. 4-42. Pattern with translational symmetry

If this biped hops on both feet at the same time, the trail will have both translational and reflective symmetry. It will also have, as an inevitable consequence, glide-reflection symmetry.

Fig. 4-43. Pattern with translational and reflective symmetry, as well as glide-reflection symmetry

If this biped walks on both feet the way a human walks, the trail will have translational symmetry and glide-reflection symmetry, but it will *not* have reflective symmetry.

Fig. 4-44. Pattern with translational and glide-reflection symmetry, but *not* reflective symmetry

All polygonal tessellations have translational symmetry. Many also have reflective symmetry and, consequently, glide-reflection symmetry. Among the latter, we can include all tessellations of regular polygons.

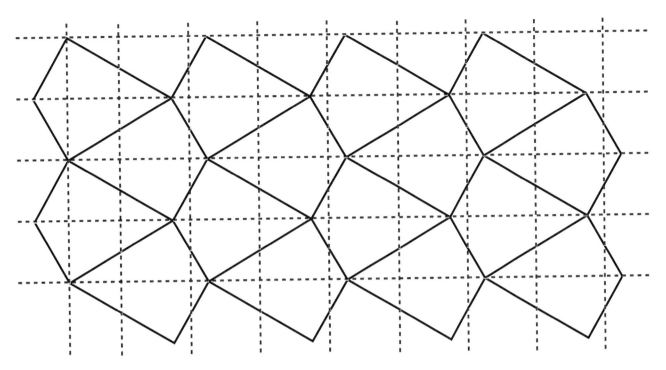

Fig. 4-45. Tessellation with glide-reflection symmetry in two directions

The nature of tessellations makes it impossible for a *polygonal* tessellation to have glide-reflection symmetry without having reflective symmetry. With this statement in mind, let's explore the tessellation of kite-shaped quadrilaterals in figure 4-45.

You will see two sets of dotted lines overlaid on the tessellation, one horizontal and the other vertical. The horizontal lines are lines of reflection. If the tessellation is reflected about any of these horizontal lines, it will coincide with itself. If it is reflected about any of these horizontal lines and then translated horizontally an appropriate distance, it will coincide with itself again. By definition, the tessellation has glide-reflection symmetry.

The tessellation does *not* have any vertical lines of reflection. However, if it is reflected about any of the vertical lines and then translated vertically an appropriate distance, it will coincide with itself. Once again, the tessellation has glide-reflection symmetry. However, the *nature* of the glide reflection in the two directions (horizontal and vertical) is quite different.

In a later chapter, we will modify a kite-shaped quadrilateral and generate a *non-polygonal* tessellation with glide-reflection symmetry but without reflective symmetry in any direction whatsoever.

Understanding the four types of symmetry presented in this chapter enables us to visualize more of the inherent underlying structure as we analyze tessellations. Additionally, knowing the four transformations—translations, rotations, reflections, and glide reflections—gives us some creative alternatives to consider when inventing designs of our own. With these transformation tools, we can create an infinitude of tessellating pattern designs. In the next chapter, we will explore a number of different techniques for creating such designs. Many of these involve transformations, either of individual design elements or entire tessellations.

Answers to Figures 4-23 through 4-30

Following are the centers of rotational symmetry in the eight semiregular tessellations:

4.8.8   two-fold rotational symmetry: midpoints of common edge of two octagons

four-fold rotational symmetry: centers of squares; centers of octagons

3.12.12   two-fold rotational symmetry: midpoints of common edges of dodecagons

three-fold rotational symmetry: centers of triangles

six-fold rotational symmetry: centers of dodecagons

3.6.3.6   two-fold rotational symmetry: vertices of triangles

three-fold rotational symmetry: centers of triangles

six-fold rotational symmetry: centers of hexagons

3.3.3.4.4   two-fold rotational symmetry: midpoints of common edge of two squares; midpoints of common edge of two triangles; center of square

4.6.12   two-fold rotational symmetry: centers of squares

three-fold rotational symmetry: centers of hexagons

six-fold rotational symmetry: centers of dodecagons

3.4.6.4   two-fold rotational symmetry: centers of squares

three-fold rotational symmetry: centers of triangles

six-fold rotational symmetry: centers of hexagons

3.3.3.3.6   two-fold rotational symmetry: midpoints of segments that are located at 60° clockwise rotations from the sides of the hexagons

three-fold rotational symmetry: centers of triangles touching three hexagons

six-fold rotational symmetry: centers of hexagons

3.3.4.3.4   two-fold rotational symmetry: midpoints of common edges of triangles; centers of squares

Answers to Figure 4-36

Pattern a: three-fold rotational symmetry; three lines reflective symmetry

Pattern b: four-fold rotational symmetry; four lines reflective symmetry

Pattern c: six-fold rotational symmetry; six lines reflective symmetry

Pattern d: no rotational symmetry; one line reflective symmetry

Pattern e: four-fold rotational symmetry; four lines reflective symmetry

Pattern f: four-fold rotational symmetry; no reflective symmetry

Pattern g: four-fold rotational symmetry; four lines reflective symmetry

Pattern h: six-fold rotational symmetry; six lines reflective symmetry

Pattern i: four-fold rotational symmetry; no reflective symmetry

Pattern j: four-fold rotational symmetry; four lines reflective symmetry

Pattern k: three-fold rotational symmetry; three lines reflective symmetry

Pattern l: two-fold rotational symmetry; two lines reflective symmetry

Pattern m: six-fold rotational symmetry; no reflective symmetry

Pattern n: four-fold rotational symmetry; no reflective symmetry

Chapter 5

TECHNIQUES FOR GENERATING TESSELLATIONS

This chapter addresses some—although by no means *all*—of the different techniques that we can use to generate tessellation designs. Many of these strategies are used in combination with one or more other techniques. They involve either sketching modifications of existing tessellations or visualizing those modifications in your mind's eye. The ideas in this chapter will give you a variety of approaches to creating your own tessellation patterns. Some of them are fundamental to creating Escher-like drawings, a topic that we discuss in detail in chapter 7.

Using Intersecting Parallel Lines

In chapter 2 we learned that any triangle, quadrilateral, or hexagon whose opposite sides are parallel and congruent will tessellate the plane by itself. One simple technique, therefore, is to use one of these three polygonal shapes as a template and trace the shape numerous times to form a tessellation. Observing patterns within such a tessellation will reveal patterns that suggest other techniques for generating tessellations. For example, we might observe that in tessellating triangles, we frequently see three sets of parallel lines. These lines are shown in figure 5-1 as black lines, red lines, and dotted lines.

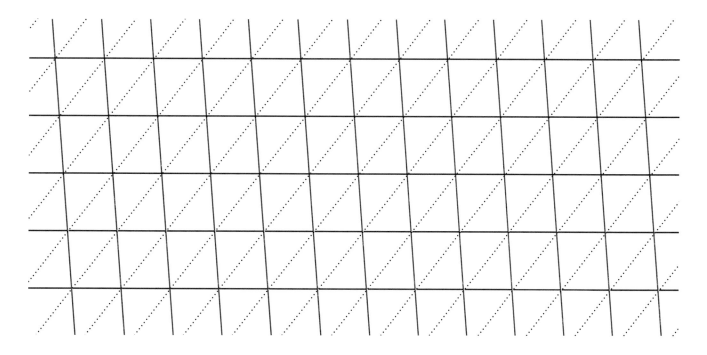

Fig. 5-1. Triangle tessellation seen as three sets of parallel lines

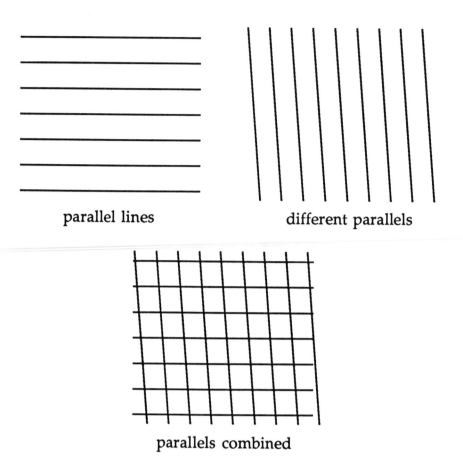

parallel lines   different parallels

parallels combined

Fig. 5-2. Two sets of parallel lines form tessellating parallelograms.

Any two sets of parallel lines will form tessellating parallelograms, as shown in figure 5-2. Adding all the diagonals in the same direction transforms those tessellating parallelograms into a pattern of tessellating triangles. Figure 5-3 demonstrates that this could be done in two different ways.

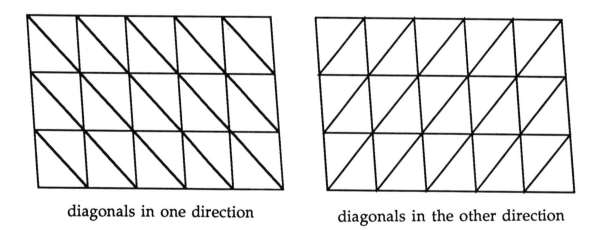

diagonals in one direction   diagonals in the other direction

Fig. 5-3. Creating tessellating triangles
from tessellating parallelograms

In figure 5-4, we see that even tessellating quadrilaterals *not* formed by intersecting parallel lines can be transformed into tessellating triangles by drawing their diagonals.

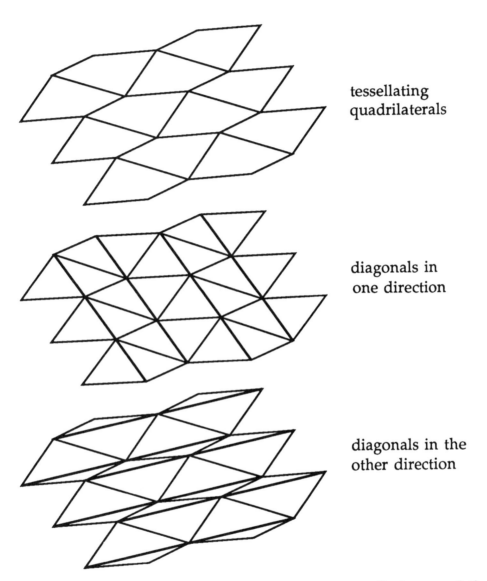

tessellating
quadrilaterals

diagonals in
one direction

diagonals in the
other direction

Fig. 5-4. Creating tessellating triangles from tessellating quadrilaterals

We can also form interesting tessellations with parallel sets of "broken" or zigzag lines. Figure 5-5 shows a broken-line pattern that we might use as a starting place. The pattern has been generated on dot paper by connecting two segments of different lengths drawn at alternating angles.

Fig. 5-5. Broken-line pattern

Repeating our broken-line pattern creates a series of parallel segments somewhat similar to a set of parallel lines.

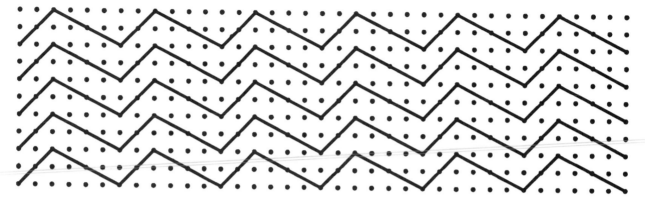

Fig. 5-6. Parallel broken line segments

When we connect the corresponding vertices, we get a configuration of tessellating parallelograms.

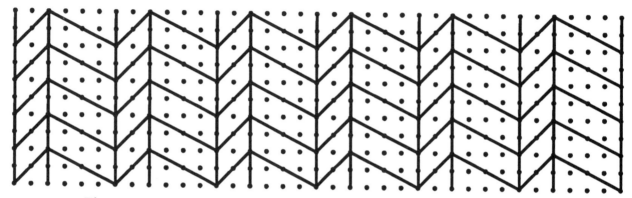

Fig. 5-7. Parallel broken line segments that intersect vertical parallel lines (forming tessellating quadrilaterals)

Alternatively, we could join the corresponding vertices of each broken line segment pattern instead of each collinear (or straight) line segment, as shown in figure 5-8. The result would be a tessellation of hexagons with opposite sides parallel and congruent.

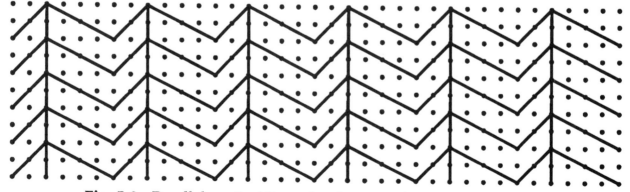

Fig. 5-8. Parallel vertical lines that intersect broken-line patterns (forming tessellating hexagons)

Let's see what happens when we use broken lines for both sets of parallels. Starting with the same horizontal broken-line pattern, we can draw a vertical set of broken-line parallels, intersecting the "point up" vertices only. This gives us a tessellation of octagons (figure 5-9). Through this approach to forming tessellations with intersecting parallel lines, we begin to sense that we could use a lattice of points to generate tessellations—which brings us to our second technique.

Fig. 5-9. Two sets of parallel broken-line patterns (forming tessellating octagons)

Creating Patterns on Dot Paper

A lattice of points spaced equally in rows and columns serves as a helpful background for designing tessellations. Often the dots are positioned to represent the vertices of tessellating squares or equilateral triangles.

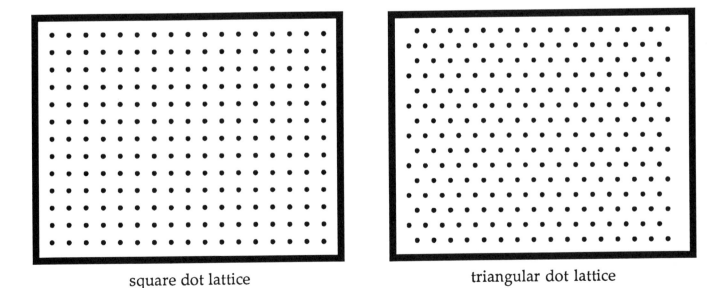

square dot lattice   triangular dot lattice

Fig. 5-10. Two types of dot paper useful for sketching tessellations

Sheets of dot paper masters are provided in the back of this book. These pages may be photocopied in quantity for use in exploring and designing tessellations by sketching patterns. Many of the techniques described later in this chapter are best approached by sketching a design initially on dot paper. Examples of typical explorations done on dot paper are shown in figures 5-11 through 5-19.

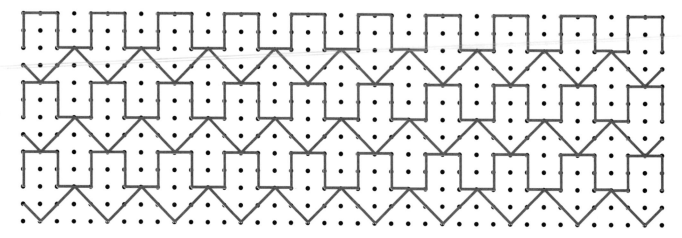

Fig. 5-11. Pattern of arrows

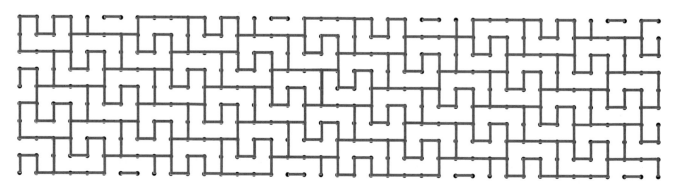

Fig. 5-12. Pattern of pentominoes

Fig. 5-13. Pattern of squares and crosses

Fig. 5-14. Pattern created by connecting the vertices of squares

Fig. 5-15. Pattern created by connecting the vertices
of two different types of square

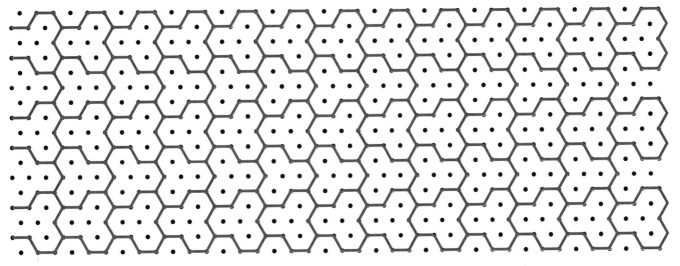

Fig. 5-16. Pattern created by combining three hexagon shapes

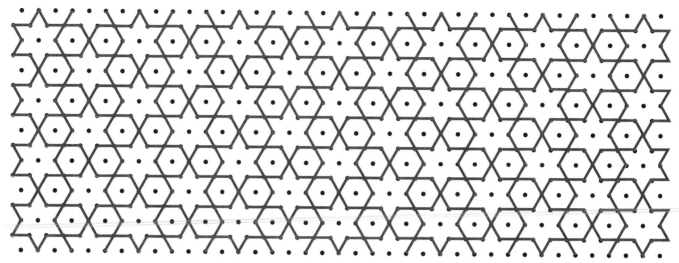

Fig. 5-17. Pattern of star polygons and hexagons

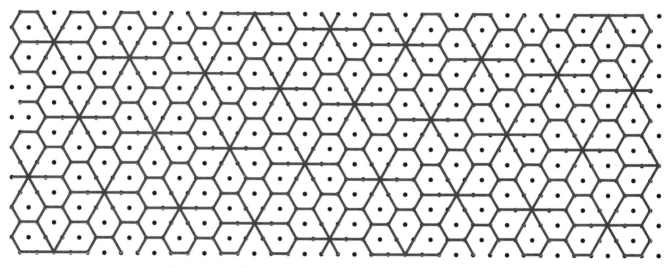

Fig. 5-18. Pattern of pentagons forming rosettes

Fig. 5-19. Pattern of identical pinwheels

Another technique for generating creative tessellation patterns is to design a basic tessellating grid pattern, then make a transparency of that grid. By moving the transparent duplication around on top of the original design, you can find new and more elaborate tessellations. Examples of designs created by this technique are shown in figures 5-20 through 5-28. As you analyze these designs, look particularly at the vertex points and note (1) their new position in relation to their original position, and (2) their relationship to key elements in the new design.

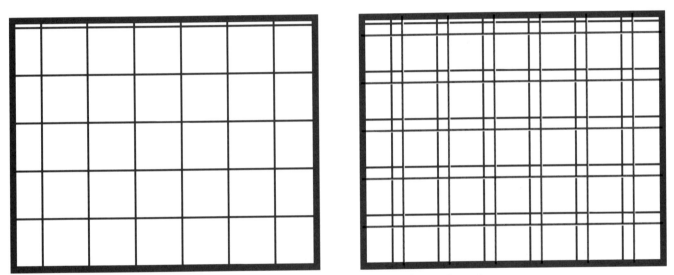

Fig. 5-20. Square grid and tessellation of overlapping squares

Fig. 5-21. Triangular grid and tessellation of overlapping triangles

Fig. 5-22. Hexagonal grid and five tessellations of overlapping hexagons

Fig. 5-23. Overlapping squares centered at a vertex point

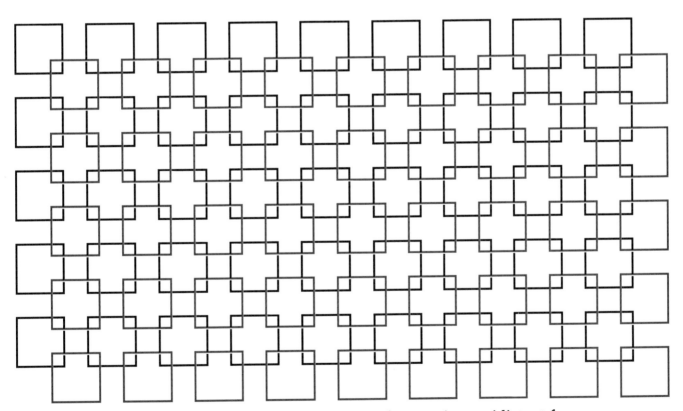

Fig. 5-24. Overlapping squares centered at a point equidistant from the square vertices

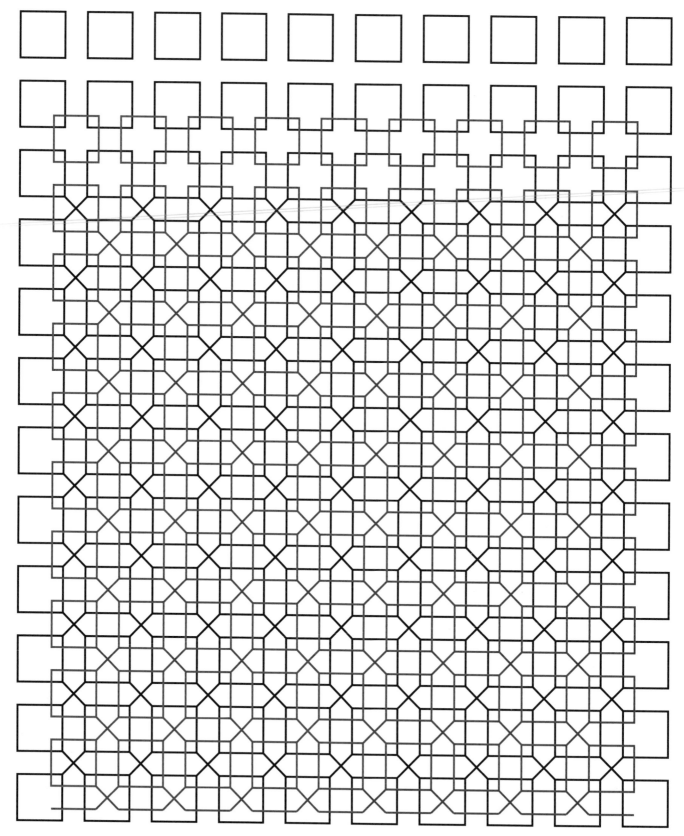

Fig. 5-25. Overlapping octagonal designs (Notice that this is an elaboration of figure 5-24, with diagonal lines connecting the vertices of adjacent squares.)

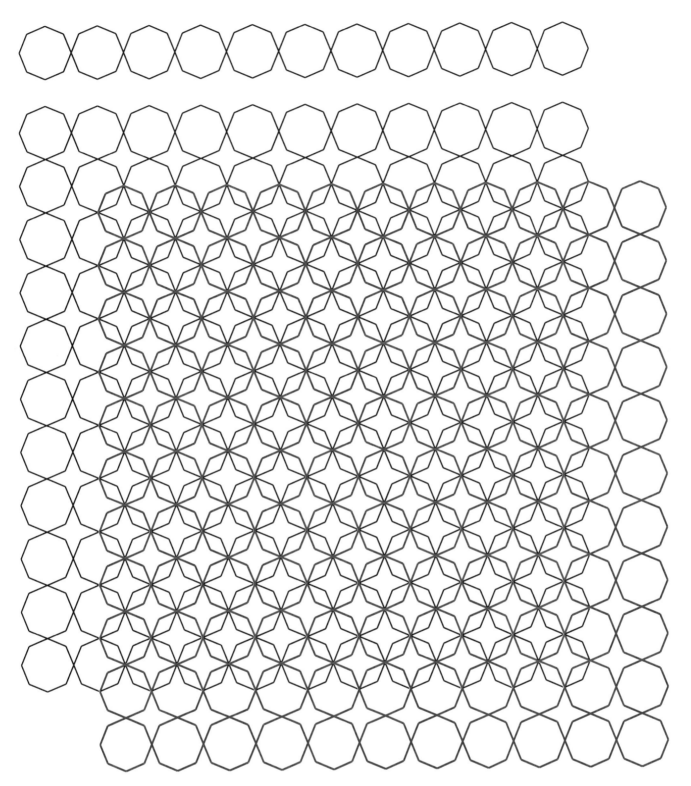

Fig. 5-26. Overlapping octagonal designs

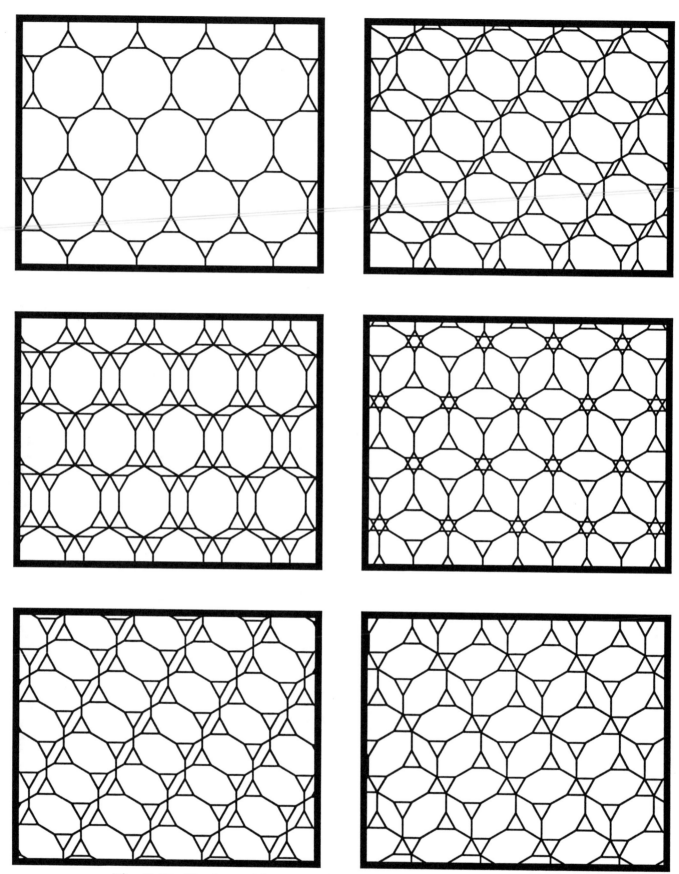

Fig. 5-27. Design with two polygonal shapes, and five variations created by overlapping the original design

Fig. 5-28. Overlapping octagonal design (one base and three overlays)

As we learned in chapter 2, a hexagon whose opposite sides are parallel and congruent will tessellate. Notice in figure 5-29 that the two identical hexagonal patterns overlap so that vertices coincide, resulting in three tessellating parallelograms.

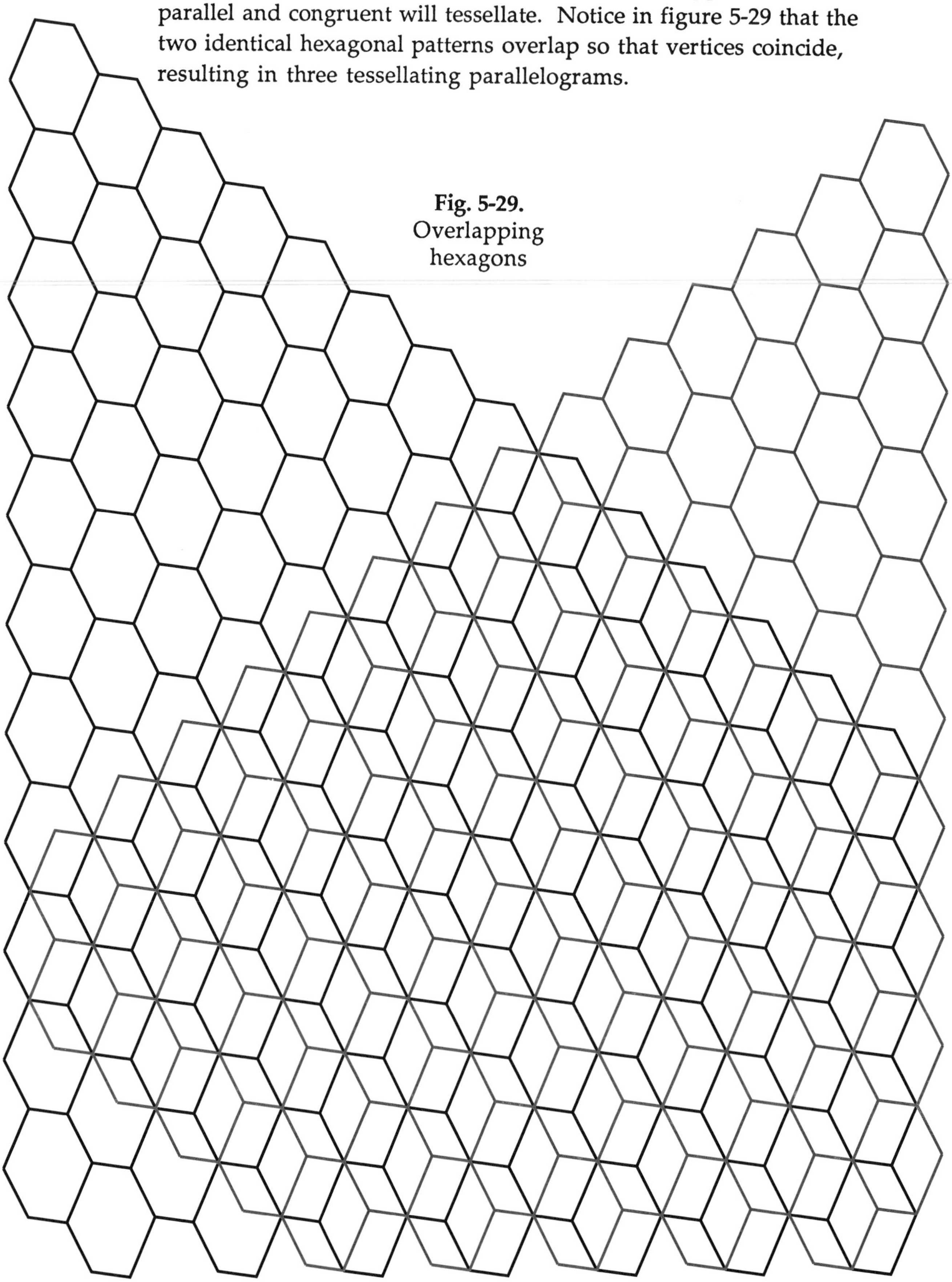

Fig. 5-29.
Overlapping
hexagons

In the following example (figure 5-30), the pattern is formed by a square grid that has been overlapped and rotated. Intersections occur at the midpoints of line segments.

Fig. 5-30. Overlapping tessellation of squares rotated to create a Pythagorean-type pattern

We just saw how rotating an entire overlapping tessellation can create an interesting new pattern (figure 5-30). In a related technique, instead of rotating an entire overlaid design, we can rotate a *single unit* of the original design. This technique is illustrated in figures 5-31 through 5-37. In figures 5-31, 5-32, and 5-33, each square from the original underlying square grid has been rotated about one of its vertices. Deleting the original underlying grid leaves an interesting pattern. In figure 5-34, each square has been rotated 30° both clockwise and counterclockwise; figure 5-35 shows an enlargement of the pattern thus created. Figures 5-36 and 5-37 show a similar approach with tessellating rhombi and hexagons.

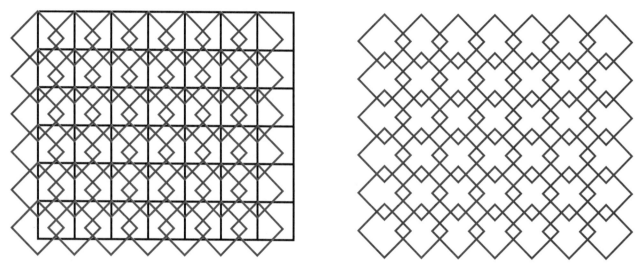

Fig. 5-31. Square rotated 45°, with and without underlying grid

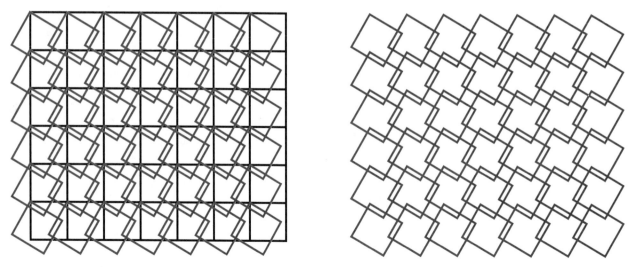

Fig. 5-32. Square rotated 30°, with and without underlying grid

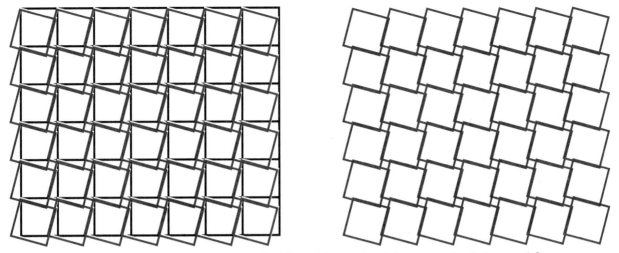

Fig. 5-33. Square rotated 15°, with and without underlying grid

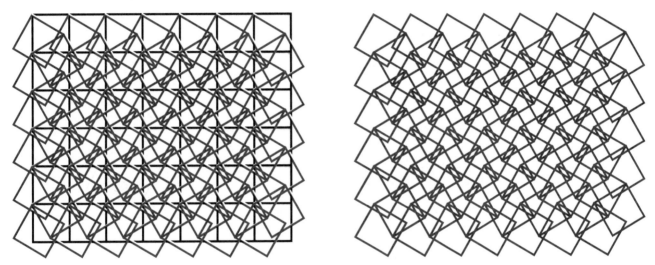

Fig. 5-34. Square rotated 30° in two directions

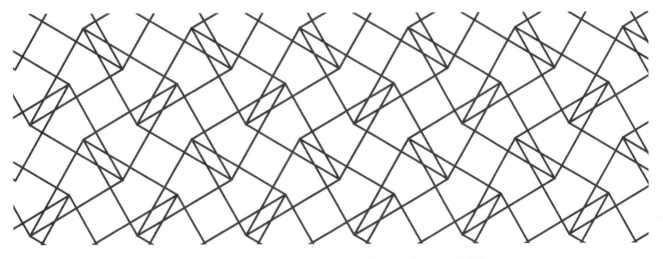

Fig 5-35. Enlarged pattern from figure 5-34

Fig. 5-36. Rhombus rotated 45°

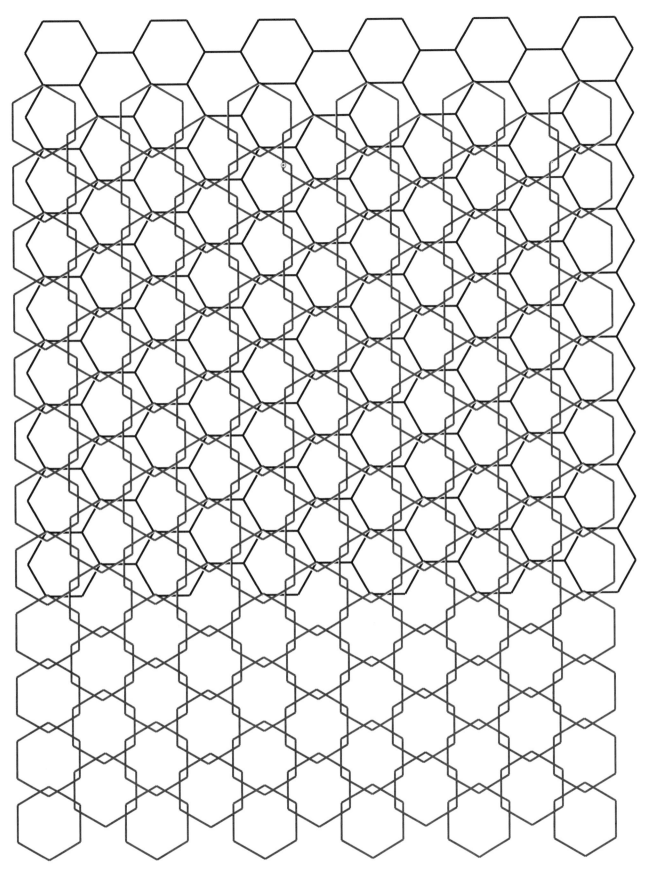

Fig. 5-37. Hexagon rotated 30°

We have seen that tessellating patterns can be created from underlying grids and lattices. We have also seen that more complex designs can be created by duplicating a design and moving it on top of itself. This next technique combines those two methods. Take a square grid, for example. First, we superimpose this grid over itself and make a horizontal translation or slide (figure 5-38). The result is a new grid having two sizes of rectangle. By connecting diagonals of the rectangles as shown in figure 5-39, we can form a tessellating quadrilateral design.

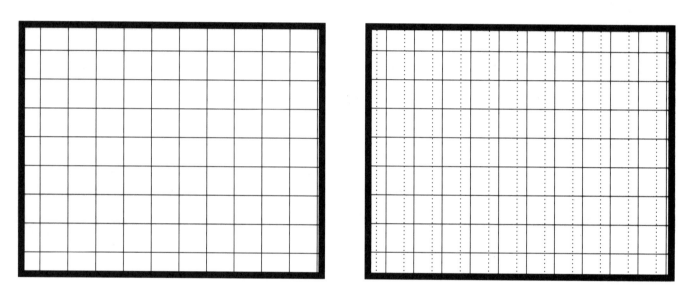

Fig. 5-38. Square grid and the same grid superimposed and translated

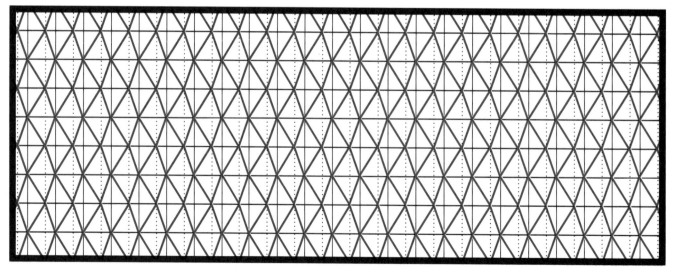

Fig. 5-39. Final tessellation on the modified grid

The same procedure is used in figures 5-40 and 5-41, although this time we begin with a parallelogram grid instead of a square grid. Another difference is that we translate the grid at an oblique angle, introducing an additional set of vertices. In the final design, notice that the tessellating quadrilateral shapes have no congruent sides.

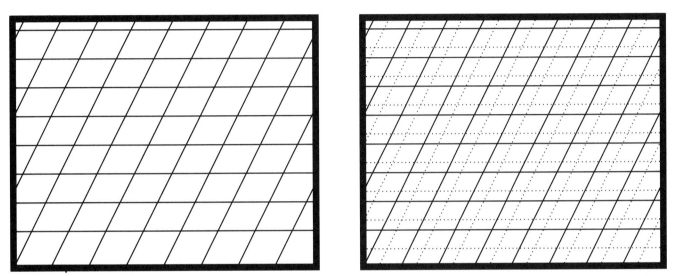

Fig. 5-40. Parallelogram grid and the same grid superimposed and translated

Fig. 5-41. Final tessellation on the modified grid

Every regular polygon has a center point called a *centroid*. This centroid is equidistant from the sides and also equidistant from the vertices. It is a center of balance in the figure.

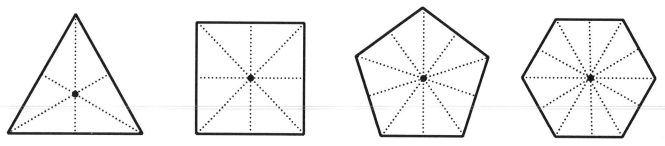

Fig. 5-42. Centroids of regular polygons

Since all regular polygons have easily located centroids, we can mark all the centroids in a tessellation of regular polygons. Connecting all these points creates a new tessellation which is the *dual* of the original tessellation. Compare figures 5-43 and 5-45; you will note that the tessellation of triangles has a dual of tessellating hexagons and vice versa. The tessellation of squares (figure 5-44) has a dual of tessellating squares, so it is called a *self-dual*.

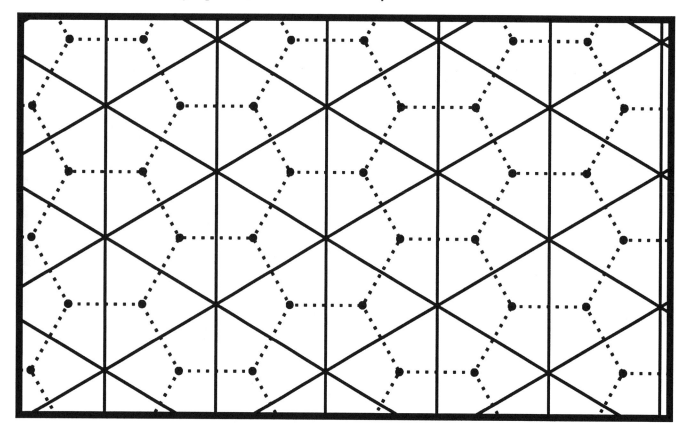

Fig. 5-43. Dual of equilateral triangles

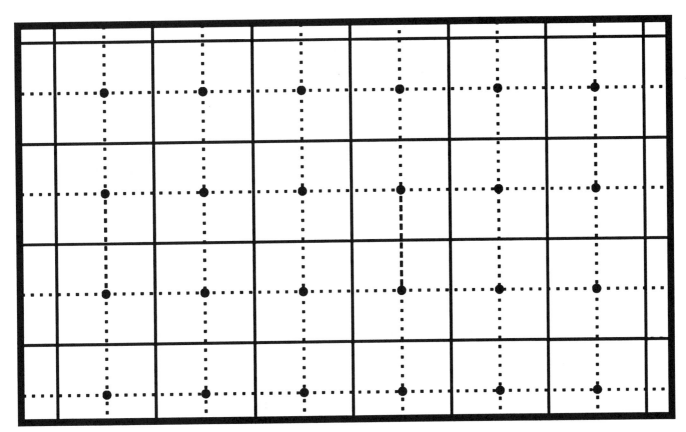

Fig. 5-44. Dual of squares

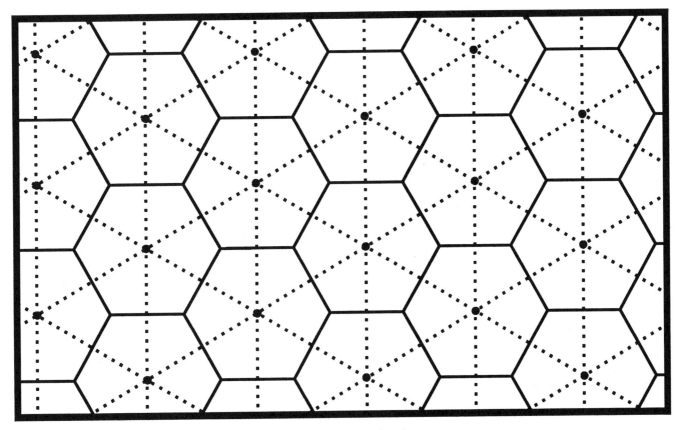

Fig. 5-45. Dual of regular hexagons

Since the eight semiregular tessellations are formed from regular polygons, we can find the centroids of each of those polygons and connect them to observe their duals. Four of these duals are shown in figures 5-46 through 5-49.

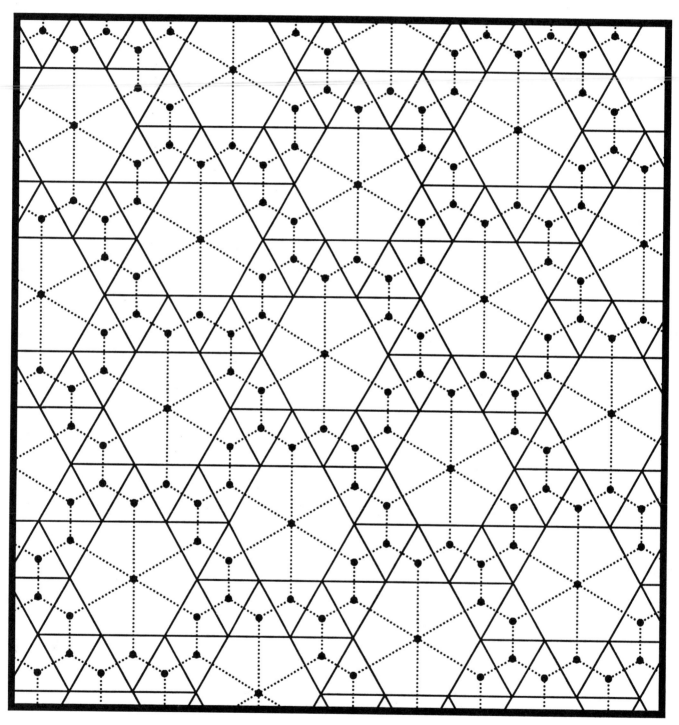

Fig. 5-46. Dual of the semiregular tessellation 3.3.3.3.6 is a tessellating pentagon.

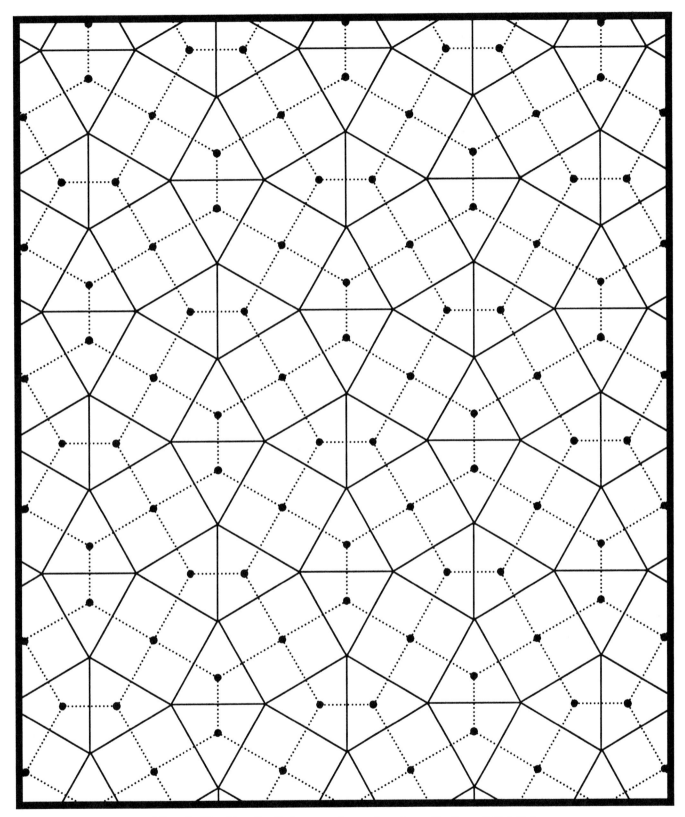

Fig. 5-47. Dual of the semiregular tessellation 3.3.4.3.4 is a tessellating pentagon.

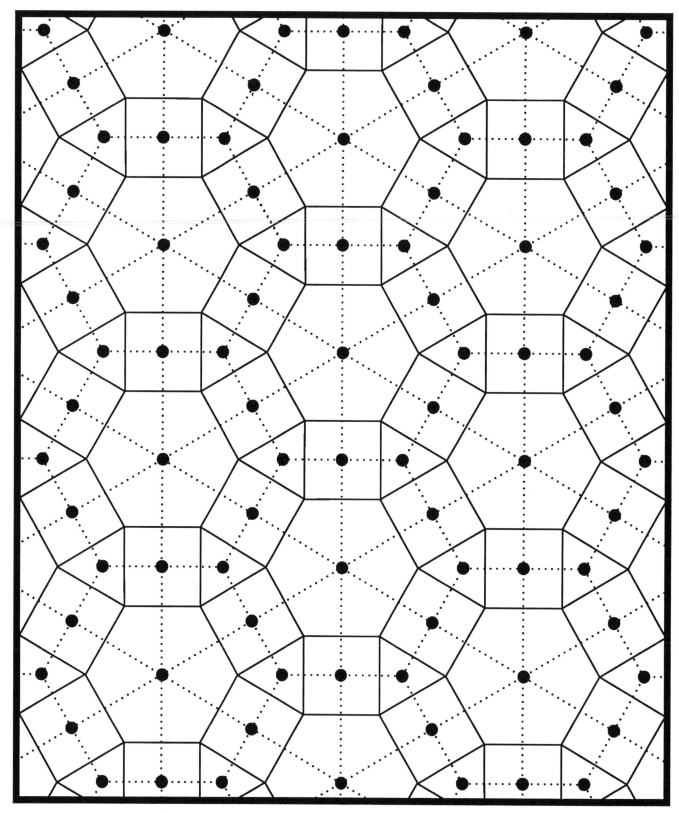

Fig. 5-48. Dual of the semiregular tessellation 3.4.6.4 is a tessellating kite.

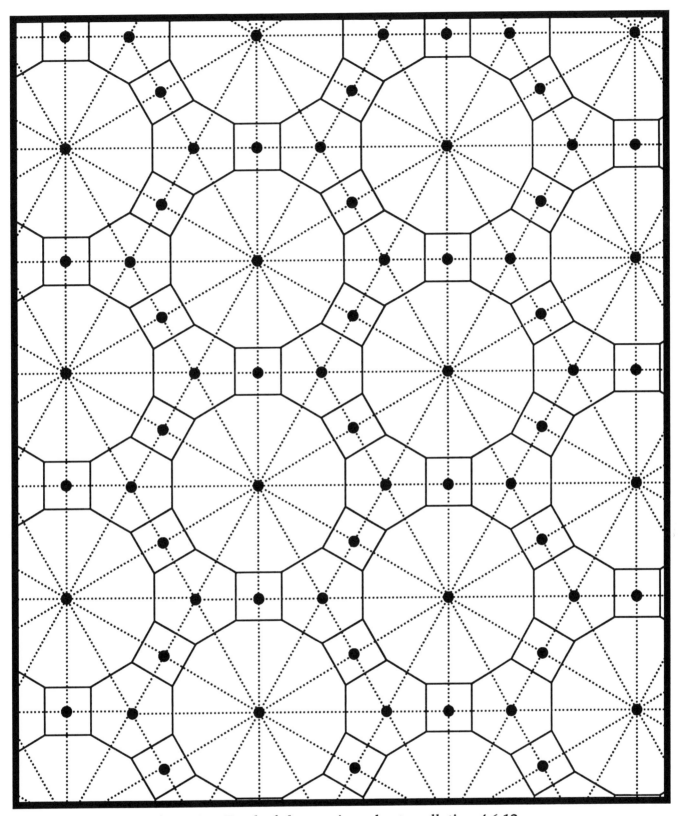

Fig. 5-49. Dual of the semiregular tessellation 4.6.12
is a tessellating right triangle.

Recall that a *centroid* is the center of balance in a polygon. We can locate the centroid of any triangle by drawing or constructing its three *medians*. A median of a triangle is a line segment that joins one vertex with the midpoint of the opposite side. The three medians of any triangle meet at a common point, the centroid. (This same approach can be used to find the centroid of every *regular* polygon, but it will not work with polygons in general. While every polygon has a center of balance, it is not always easily found by construction methods.)

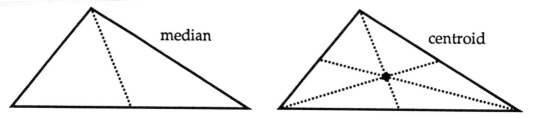

Fig. 5-50. Finding the centroid of any triangle

The tessellating triangle shown in figure 5-51 has its centroids connected to form a dual of tessellating hexagons. Figure 5-52 shows another triangle tessellating in two different arrangements. Notice that the duals for each arrangement are different.

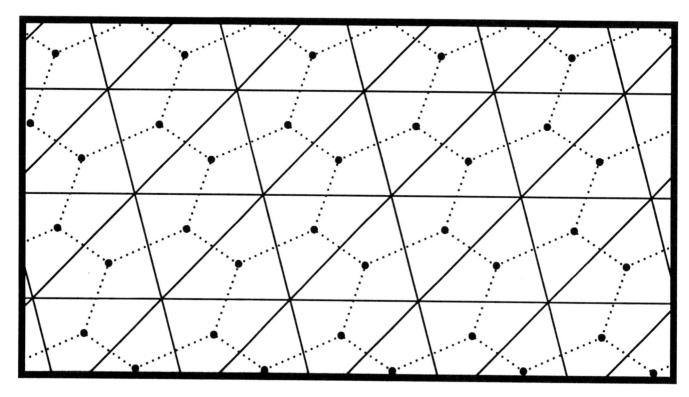

Fig. 5-51. Dual of tessellating triangles

Fig. 5-52. Two different tessellations of the same triangle and their hexagonal duals

Quadrilaterals have the special property that lines joining the midpoints of their four sides form a parallelogram. Examples of this property are illustrated in figure 5-53 with common types of quadrilaterals.

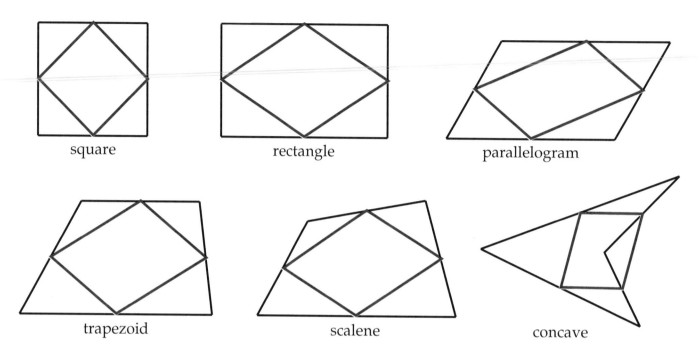

square   rectangle   parallelogram

trapezoid   scalene   concave

Fig. 5-53. Parallelograms joining midpoints of sides

Connecting the midpoints of tessellating quadrilaterals creates a grid similar to a dual. As with a dual, this new grid forms a different tessellation pattern. Examples of this technique are shown in figures 5-54 through 5-57.

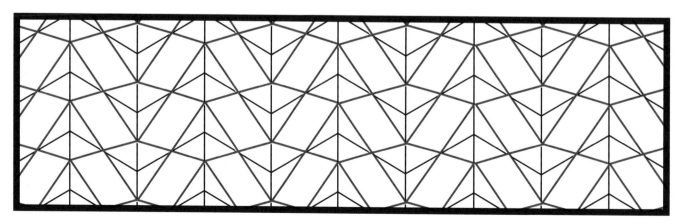

Fig. 5-54. Connected midpoints of a tessellating parallelogram form a two-shape tessellation.

Fig. 5-55. Connected midpoints of a tessellating rhombus form a "stretched" semiregular tessellation.

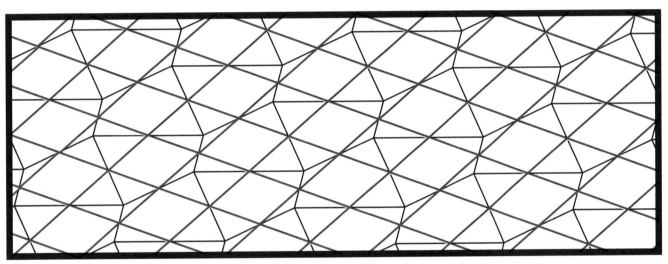

Fig. 5-56. Connected midpoints of a tessellating scalene quadrilateral form a grid of parallel lines.

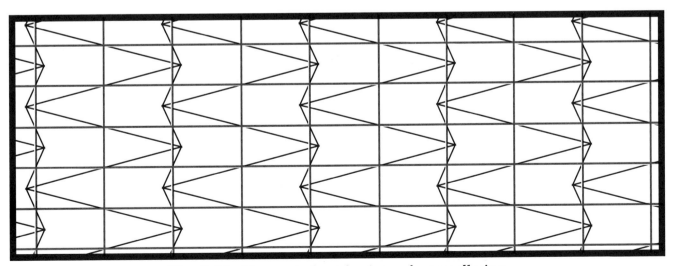

Fig. 5-57. Connected midpoints of a tessellating concave quadrilateral form a grid of rectangles.

As you can see, connecting the midpoints of tessellating quadrilaterals generates quite different types of patterns, depending on the shape of the quadrilateral. An interesting question for you to explore would be: Which types of quadrilateral tessellations will produce sets of parallel lines using this method?

We can also use this technique (connecting midpoints of sides) with other tessellating shapes. This is what we have done in figure 5-58, starting with one of the semiregular tessellations and connecting midpoints to generate a new design.

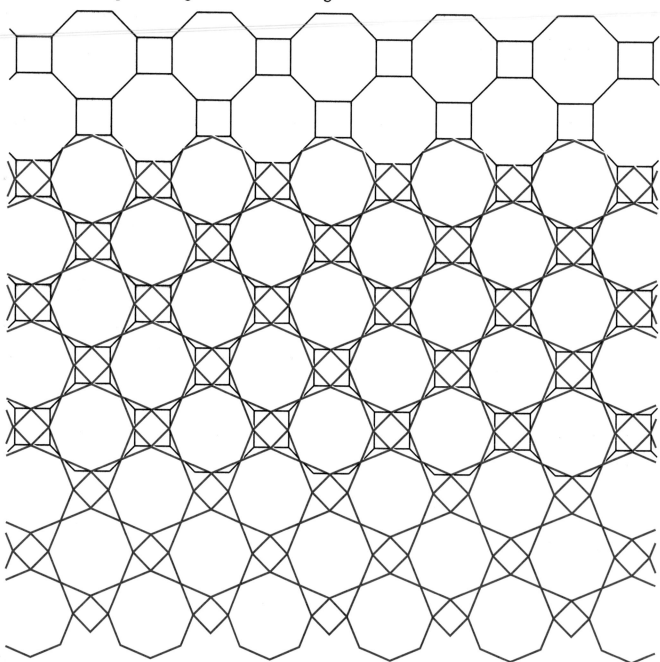

Fig. 5-58. Design formed by connecting midpoints of sides of the semiregular tessellation 4.8.8

The two techniques just described—creating duals and connecting midpoints—are quite similar, in that the centroids and midpoints of the original tessellations become the vertices of new designs. We can extend this idea to include any other points systematically chosen in a pattern; for example, a point located at the intersection of two diagonals of one of the elements of a tessellation would appear at the same location throughout the pattern. Such points could become the vertex points of a new design. The possibilities for generating new designs with this technique are endless. We will expand on this idea later when we discuss the technique "dissecting shapes."

Choosing Compatible Shapes

Compatible shapes could be defined as shapes whose sides and/or angles are either congruent or multiples of one another, and whose angles contain numbers of degrees that together, in some combination, total 360°. An excellent example of compatible shapes can be found in figure 3-18 (page 52), the 21 arrangements of regular polygon combinations that fill the space around a point. Compatible shapes need not always be regular polygons, though. Some other examples are shown in figure 5-59.

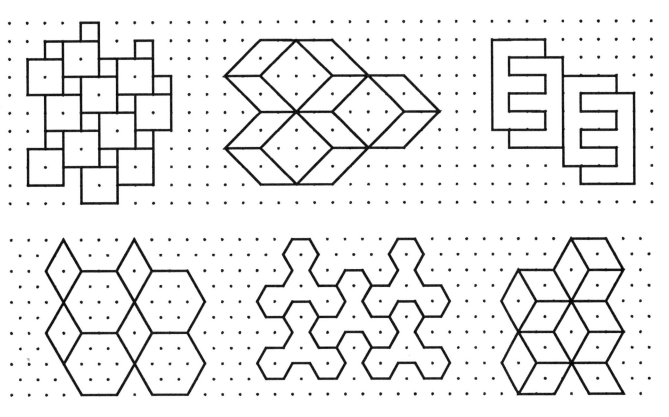

Fig. 5-59. Compatible shapes

Another example of compatible shapes that are helpful in creating tessellation designs are the manipulative models called *pattern blocks*. Originally developed at EDC in Boston by Bill Hull, pattern blocks are colored blocks of wood, plastic, or paper in six different compatible shapes (figure 5-60). Three of the shapes are regular polygons: the equilateral triangle, the square, and the regular hexagon. The other three shapes are an isosceles trapezoid (half of a regular hexagon) and two rhombi. All six shapes tessellate by themselves, and many other tessellation patterns can be created with combinations of two or more of the six shapes.

Pattern blocks are valuable tessellation tools for all ages, but they are particularly useful for young children who have yet to develop precise drawing techniques and the patience required to create patterns on paper. All the pattern block pieces have congruent edges, with the exception of the base of the trapezoid, which has a length twice that of the other pattern block edges. The angles of the shapes are conveniently either 30°, 60°, 90°, or 120°.

Fig. 5-60. Pattern block shapes serve as tessellation tools.

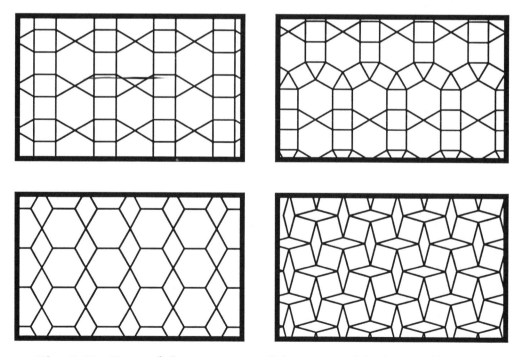

Fig. 5-61. Four of the many possible pattern block tessellations

In discussing compatible shapes, we must not overlook identical shapes. For example, perfectly congruent shapes like the brick-shaped rectangles shown in figure 5-62 can be termed compatible. They have compatible angles (all 90°), and their side lengths are in the convenient ratio of 2 to 1. The compatibility of these shapes enables us to create several different tessellating patterns.

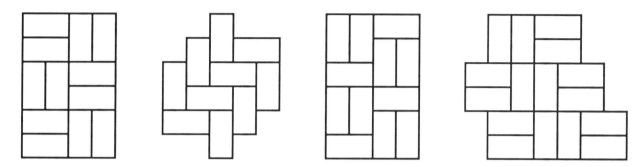

Fig. 5-62. Brick patterns formed by congruent rectangles

There's another way to create tessellations with congruent compatible shapes. Imagine that you have a number of square tiles of a single size; that is, all the tiles are congruent. Obviously you could create a regular tessellation with such tiles. You could also position them variously as shown in figure 5-63—translating (sliding) them along their sides to make several different tessellations, thinking of the gaps between the tiles as white squares of a smaller size. Can you visualize that an infinite number of different patterns could be made in this manner?

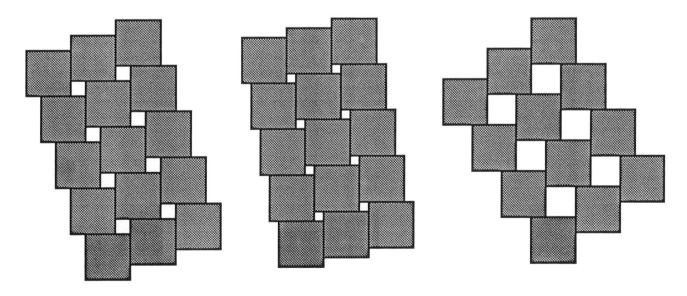

Fig. 5-63. Congruent squares creating patterns with smaller "gap" squares

We can combine congruent equilateral triangles in much the same way, starting with a regular tessellation, then sliding the triangles along their edges. Notice that the gaps in this case (figure 5-64) are hexagonal rather than triangular, but they are still compatible shapes.

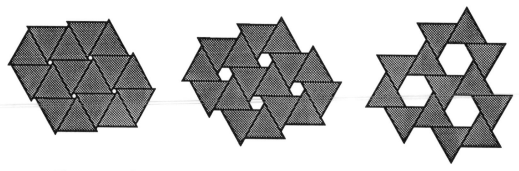

Fig. 5-64. Congruent equilateral triangles creating patterns with compatible "gap" hexagons

We could also start with the regular triangle tessellation and remove alternating triangles until we have a design of only "point up" triangles with "point down" triangular gaps. Then, when we slide the triangles along their edges, we create new patterns like those shown in figure 5-65.

Fig. 5-65. Equilateral triangles creating patterns with smaller "gap" triangles

If we start with a tessellation of regular hexagons, translating them along their sides creates compatible triangular gaps and a wide variety of new patterns.

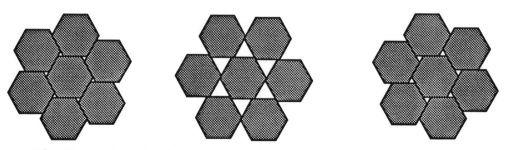

Fig. 5-66. Regular hexagons creating patterns with compatible "gap" triangles

Some designs based on compatible shapes can be modified into new designs by sliding an entire row or column of shapes. For examples of this, see figure 3-25, page 58. We can also modify a design significantly by rotating a group of shapes within a tessellation, as we have done in figure 5-67. Being able to visualize combinations of shapes that form larger symmetric shapes allows us to imagine the modifications that will create new designs.

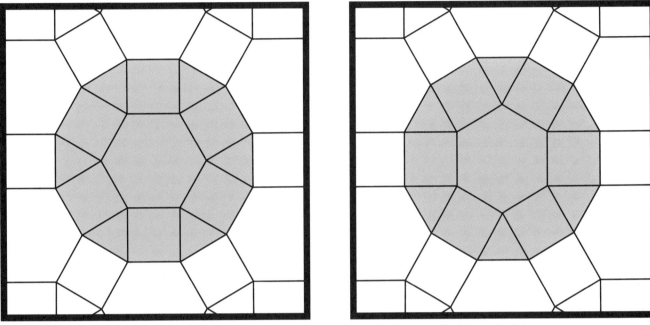

Fig. 5-67. Original position for group of shapes (left) and the same group rotated to a new position (right)

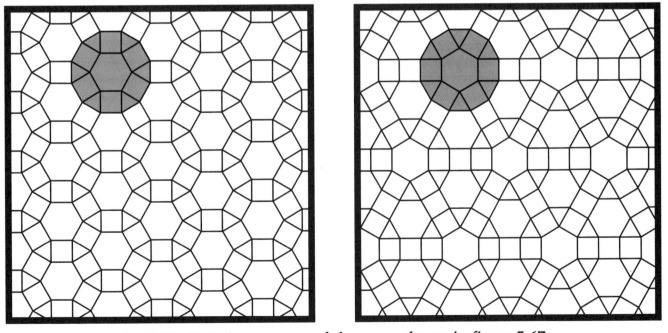

Fig. 5-68. Rotating a group of shapes as shown in figure 5-67 transforms semiregular tessellation 3.4.6.4. into a new design.

Once we have a completed tessellation, that pattern can serve as the basis for creating other designs. By combining two or more adjacent shapes in the pattern (and deleting some line segments), we can create new shapes that tessellate. Some examples of this technique are shown in figures 5-69 through 5-74.

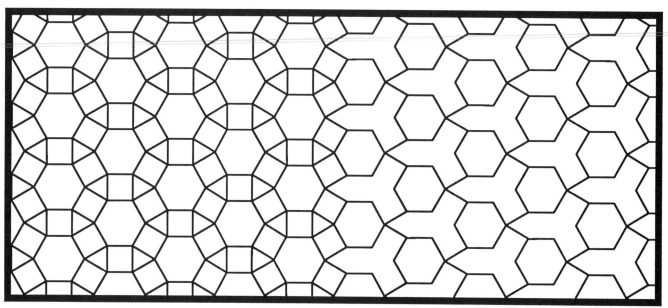

Fig. 5-69. Combining the squares and triangles of semiregular tessellation 3.4.6.4

Fig. 5-70. Combining shapes in semiregular tessellation 3.3.3.3.6 to form a star pattern

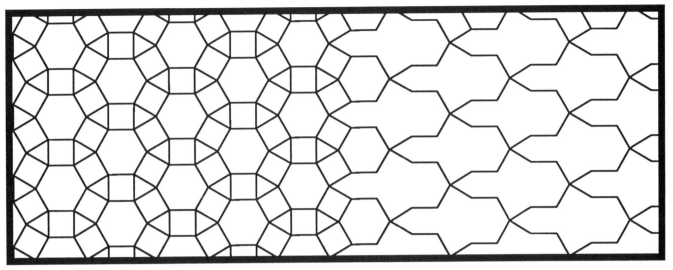

Fig. 5-71. An alternative way of combining the shapes of 3.4.6.4

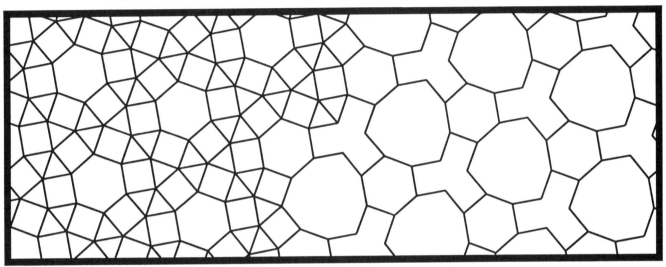

Fig. 5-72. Combining squares and triangles to create a new three-shape design

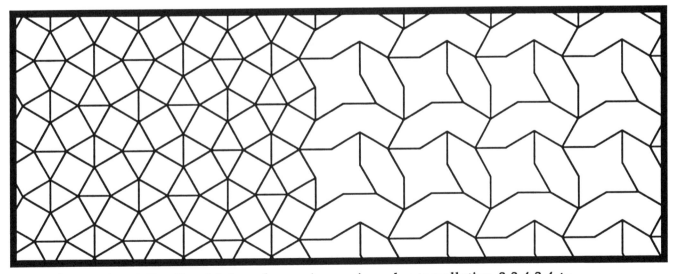

Fig. 5-73. Combining shapes in semiregular tessellation 3.3.4.3.4 to form a star pattern

Fig. 5-74. Transition tessellation shows a few possible combinations of smaller shapes into larger shapes

Dissecting Shapes

An existing tessellation can also be turned into a new design by dividing one or more of the pattern's shapes into smaller shapes. Such dissections will most frequently divide a shape into two or more congruent parts. Examples of this technique appear in figures 5-75 through 5-79.

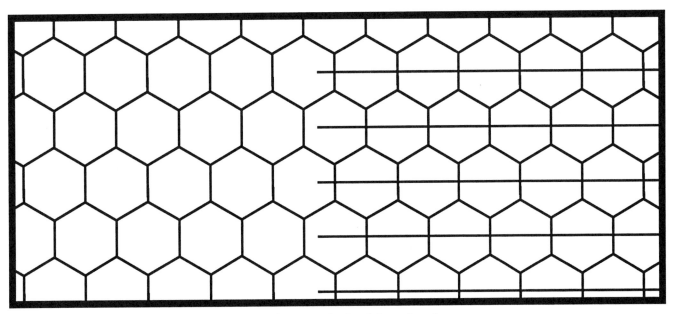

Fig. 5-75. Design made by bisecting hexagons

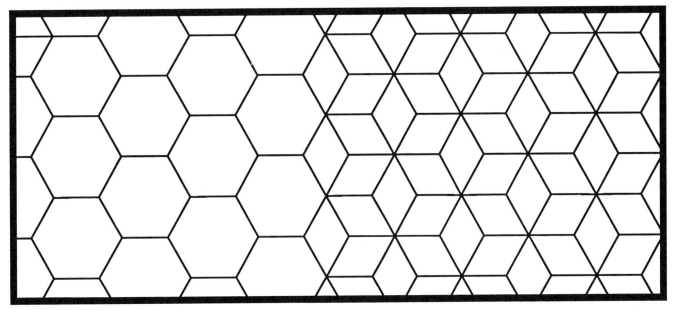

Fig. 5-76. Design made by trisecting hexagons

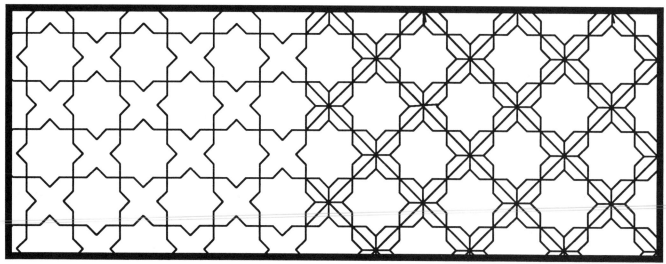

Fig. 5-77. Drawing diagonals dissects these shapes into eight equal parts, creating a new design.

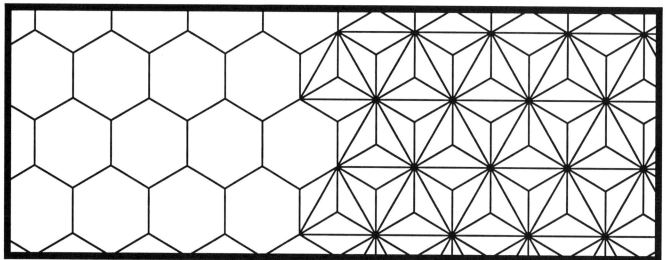

Fig. 5-78. Dividing hexagons into triangles, then trisecting the large triangle in each unit creates this star pattern.

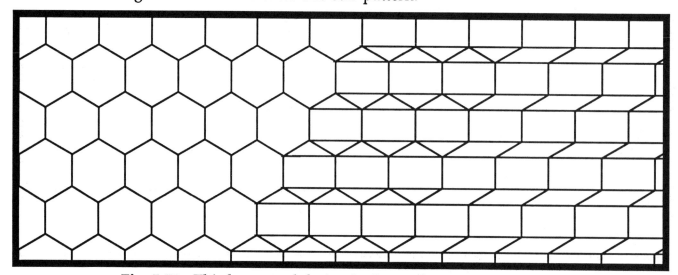

Fig. 5-79. This hexagonal design is changed to stair steps first by dissection, then by combining shapes.

Still another technique for generating tessellations that have aesthetic properties is to create unit cells. Unit cells are often seen in ceramic tiles. Most often these tiles are square. A tile by itself may not present a very interesting design; however, when several such tiles are combined to form a tessellation, surprising patterns appear. Sometimes the process may be reversed; that is, a tessellation may be designed first by some other technique, then divided into the practical, square-cell configuration. For example, we might have first created the basic overall star pattern in figure 5-80 using dot paper, then discovered the unit cell (shown above the tessellation) by connecting centroids of the stars. Unit cells frequently contain more than one type of symmetry. Some typical designs are illustrated in figures 5-80 through 5-85. You may enjoy designing some unit cells of your own.

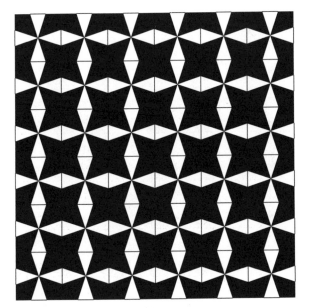

Fig. 5-80

Fig. 5-81

Fig. 5-82

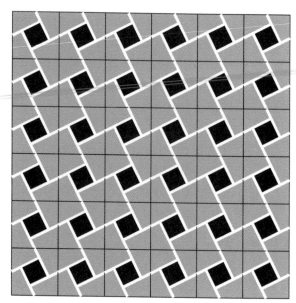

Fig. 5-83

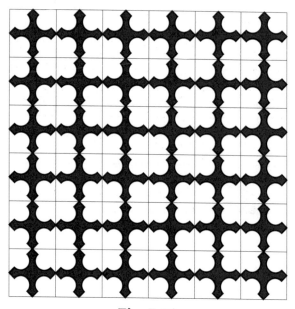

Fig. 5-84

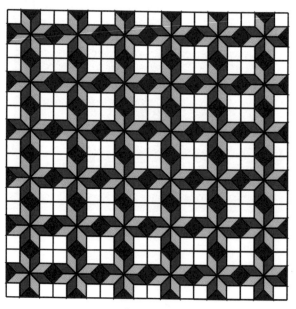

Fig. 5-85

Modifying by Translation

As we discussed in chapter 4, a *translation* is a slide on a plane along the path of a straight line. If we translate a line in a plane, it is not rotated. In figures 5-86 and 5-87, lines have been translated from one side of the parallelogram to the other. Note that *no rotation* has taken place. The process is broken down into four steps in figure 5-86. We start with a parallelogram (step 1); modify one side (step 2); translate (slide) the modified line to the opposite, parallel, congruent side (step 3); and finally, delete the original sides (step 4). The resulting shape tessellates the plane, as shown.

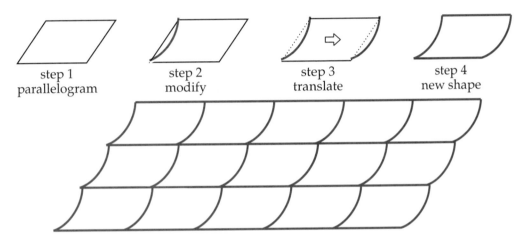

step 1
parallelogram

step 2
modify

step 3
translate

step 4
new shape

Fig. 5-86. Tessellation formed by modification, then translation

Figure 5-87 shows the tessellation of a parallelogram with *both* pairs of opposite sides modified. The steps show the modification of the second set of opposite sides, assuming the modification shown in figure 5-86 has already occurred.

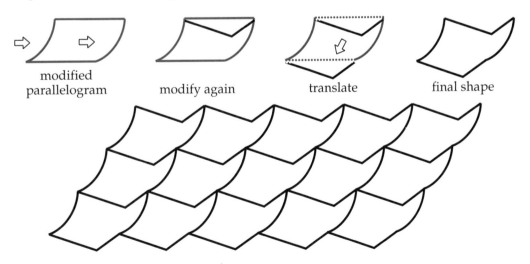

modified
parallelogram

modify again

translate

final shape

Fig. 5-87. Tessellation formed by modifying both sets of sides

In this technique of modifying one side of a parallelogram and translating the modification to the opposite side, the modification sometimes crosses the original side of the parallelogram—that is, it is drawn both outside and inside the original shape. Figure 5-88 shows modifications made by line segments that zigzag on both sides of the original line; figure 5-89 shows that the procedure works with curves as well.

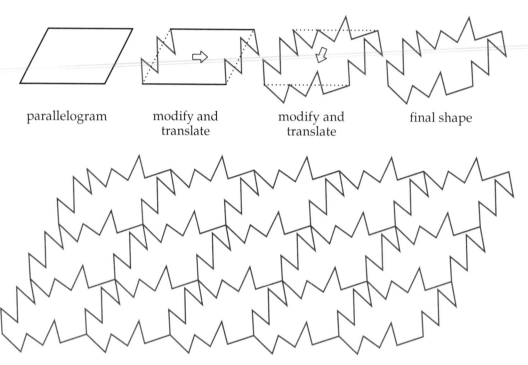

parallelogram   modify and translate   modify and translate   final shape

Fig. 5-88. Tessellation formed by broken line modifications

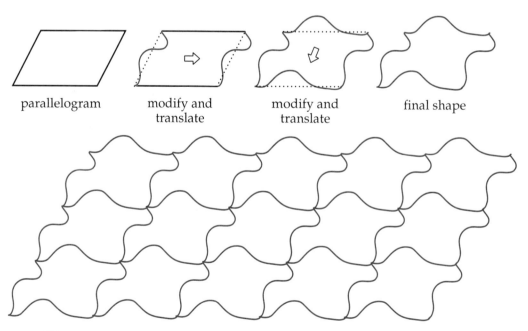

parallelogram   modify and translate   modify and translate   final shape

Fig. 5-89. Tessellation formed by modifications with curves

Although we have been looking at parallelograms up to now, modifying by translation also works with other shapes. Recall from chapters 2 and 3 that hexagons whose opposite sides are parallel and congruent will tessellate. Using the technique of modifying a line and translating it to the opposite side, we can change three pairs of sides. An example of the modification of a tessellating hexagon is shown in figure 5-90. This is one of the techniques we build on in creating Escher-like drawings, explained in more detail in chapter 7.

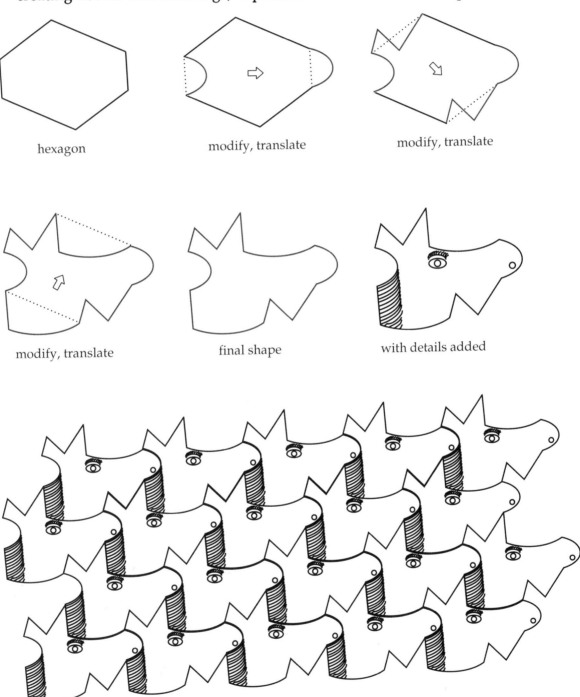

hexagon   modify, translate   modify, translate

modify, translate   final shape   with details added

Fig. 5-90. Tessellation of hexagon modified by translations

In order to translate a modified line from one side of a polygon to another, the two sides involved must be parallel and congruent. That is why we avoided triangles in discussing the previous technique, focusing instead on quadrilaterals and hexagons. There is, however, another good technique that allows us to change tessellating triangles to other shapes that tessellate. It works for some other polygons as well. The technique is this: We modify one or more half-sides of the triangle, then *rotate* that modification 180° around the midpoint of the side. Figure 5-91 shows an example of this type of modification.

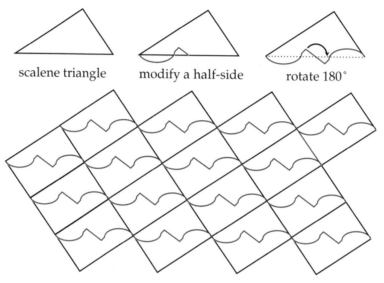

scalene triangle   modify a half-side   rotate 180°

Fig. 5-91. Tessellation of modified triangles

The shape tessellating in figure 5-91 has two remaining straight sides. Figure 5-92 shows how we can take that shape and modify one additional side by rotation about its midpoint.

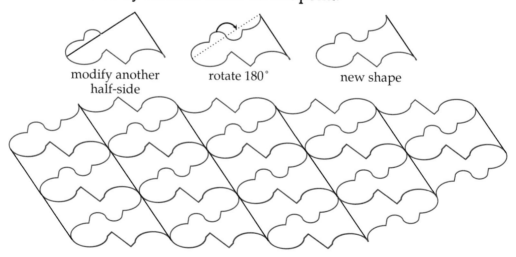

modify another   rotate 180°   new shape
half-side

Fig. 5-92. Further modification of the shape shown in figure 5-91

Naturally, we can also modify the third and final side of the triangle by the same process, as is shown in figure 5-93.

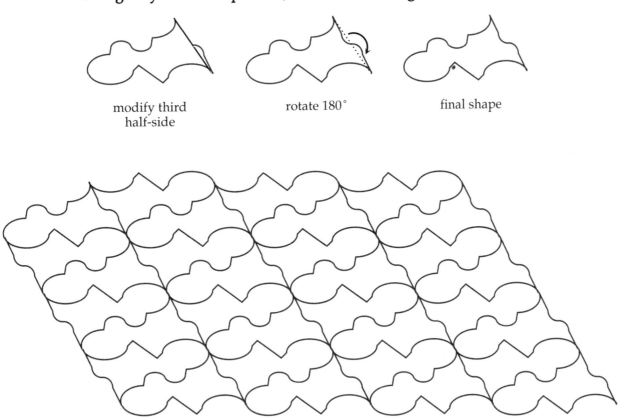

modify third
half-side

rotate 180°

final shape

Fig. 5-93. All three sides of original scalene triangle modified by rotation

The nice thing about this technique of modifying a tessellating polygon by rotation at its midpoints is that the polygon need not have special properties of parallelism or congruence. Since the modification of the half-line can be performed on either side of any line, this technique gives us lots of freedom and flexibility.

We know that every quadrilateral tessellates. Using "modifying by rotation at midpoints," we can turn any tessellating quadrilateral into another shape that also tessellates, just by changing one or more sides. In figure 5-94, we start with a scalene quadrilateral and modify all its sides by rotation about a midpoint. As is often the case, the final shape looks very dissimilar to the original, yet the areas of the final modified shape and the original quadrilateral are exactly the same. You can see that although the area changes when we modify the half-side, this change is balanced by the corresponding change after we rotate the modification 180°.

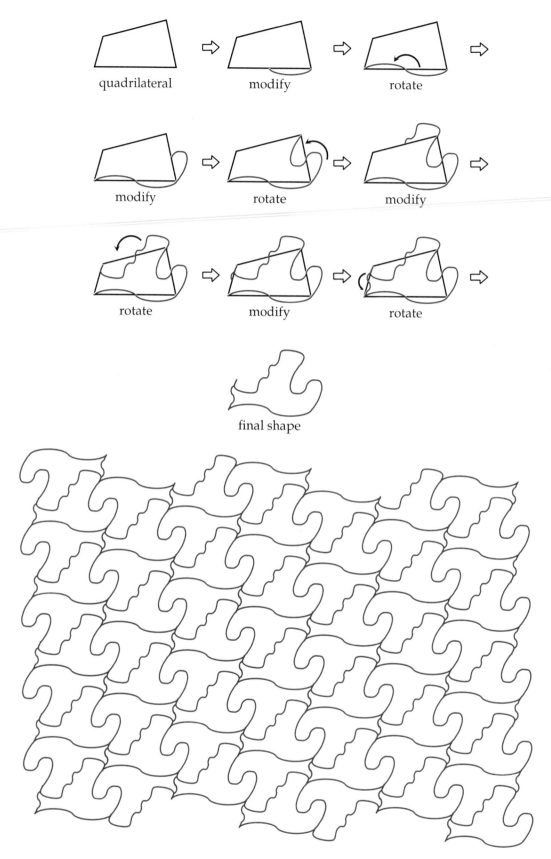

quadrilateral

modify

rotate

modify

rotate

modify

rotate

modify

rotate

final shape

Fig. 5-94. Each side of the quadrilateral is modified by altering the line from a vertex to the midpoint; then the modification is rotated 180° about the midpoint. The resulting shape tessellates.

Figure 5-95 shows some special symmetrical modifications and rotations of a half-side of a square and the resulting tessellation in each case. One modification is a semicircle; the other is a half-square.

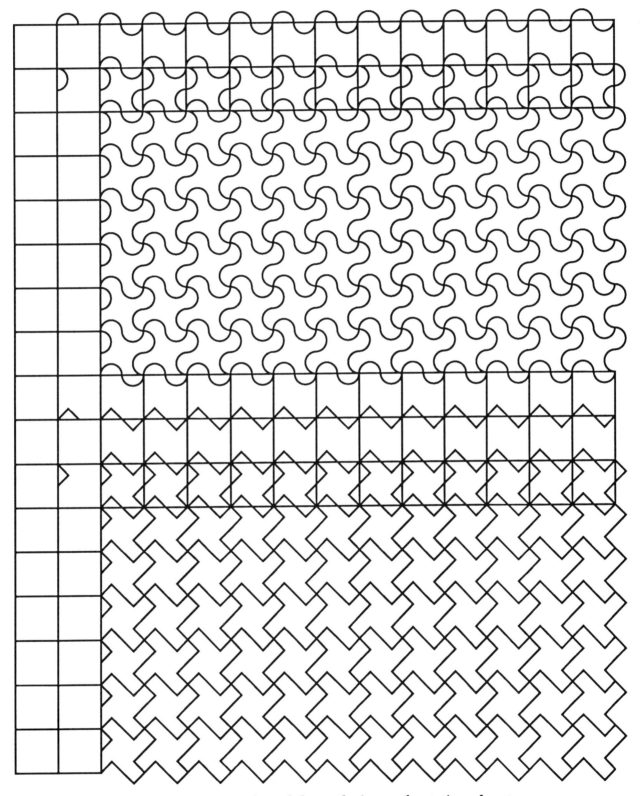

Fig. 5-95. Two examples of the technique of rotating about a midpoint, starting with a square

The technique of modifying a half-line and rotating it 180° about the midpoint of a side, which works well with triangles and quadrilaterals, will *not* work with tessellating hexagons. Recall from chapter 2 the necessary conditions for tessellating hexagons: opposite sides are congruent and parallel. Since opposite sides must coincide, they cannot have *different* modifications. In figure 5-96, we modify each half-side of a hexagon and rotate each modification 180° about the midpoint. As you can see, the resulting shape does not tessellate.

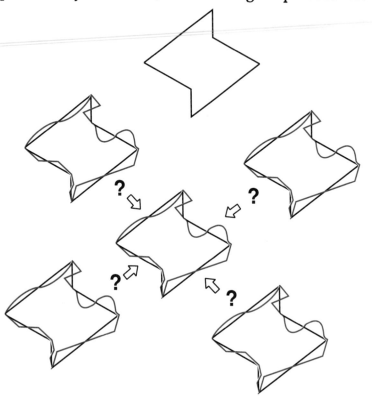

Fig. 5-96. Modifying all sides of special hexagons produces a figure that will not tessellate.

Rotating Modified Sides

In this final technique, we will modify an entire side of a triangle, then rotate it to a side that has the same length. This limits us to isosceles triangles (remember that an equilateral triangle is isosceles). Modifying an entire side of an equilateral triangle, then rotating that modification to an adjacent side will produce a new shape that tessellates. An example combining the modification of a full-side rotation and a half-side rotation is shown in figure 5-97. Notice that this tessellation contains three-fold rotational symmetry at one point and six-fold symmetry at a different point. We will refer to more symmetries in tessellations in the chapter on drawing Escher-like designs.

Fig. 5-97. Tessellation created by two types of rotation

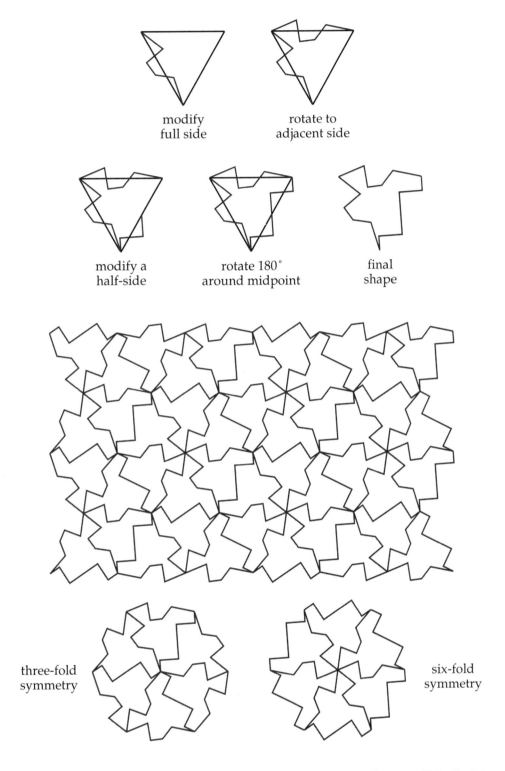

modify
full side

rotate to
adjacent side

modify a
half-side

rotate 180°
around midpoint

final
shape

three-fold
symmetry

six-fold
symmetry

Since, when we use this technique, we rotate the modified side of a triangle to an adjacent side, clearly the triangle must be at least isosceles. Further exploration will reveal that the technique always produces a tessellation with equilateral triangles, but not necessarily with isosceles triangles.

Fig. 5-98. Tessellation created by rotating modified sides of a square

Modifying an entire side of a square and rotating it to an adjacent side will produce a tessellation (figure 5-98). However, if the quadrilateral has four congruent sides but is *not* a square, difficulties arise. In figure 5-99, we modify the sides of a rhombus and rotate each modification to an adjacent side. As you can see, the resulting shape does not tessellate.

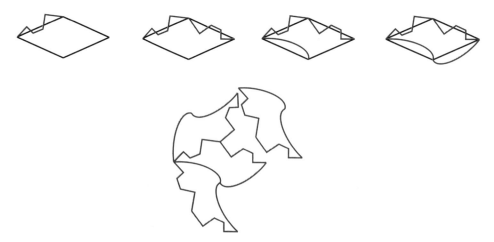

Fig. 5-99. Rotating sides of a non-square rhombus creates non-tessellating shapes.

Figure 5-100 shows a regular hexagon with sides modified and then rotated to an adjacent side, producing a shape that tessellates. As with triangles and quadrilaterals, this would not work with a nonregular hexagon. When our original figure is a regular polygon, this technique creates a tessellation, but when the shapes are not regular, a tessellation is not assured. Using rotation of modified sides will be discussed further in chapter 7.

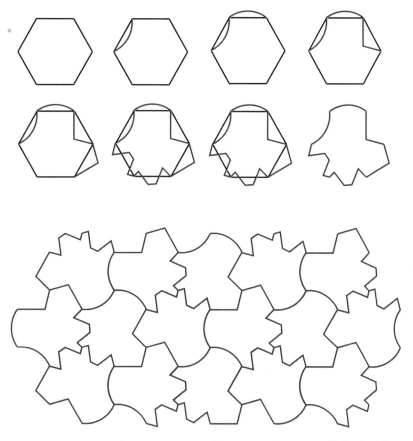

Fig. 5-100. Tessellation created by rotating modified sides of a regular hexagon

As mentioned at the beginning of this chapter, the 14 techniques presented here do not include all the known ways of generating shapes that tessellate. They are, however, the most common and the easiest to use.

As you experiment with the various techniques, be aware that special effects such as coloring or shading can enhance the appearance of your designs. Some designs create the illusion of having three dimensions, and you can select colors or shades that will strengthen this illusion. Patterns containing special symmetries may reveal those symmetries more clearly if you give some preliminary thought to the selection and number of different colors you use.

There are currently available for the personal computer a number of drawing programs that offer the basic tools of transformational geometry. With tools such as *reflect, rotate, reduce, enlarge, copy, translate,* and *sheer,* you can produce beautiful and accurate tessellation drawings in surprisingly short periods of time.

In the next two chapters we will show how to apply many of the techniques just discussed. You will find that often the same design can be created in more than one way; you will also see that in many cases, we create a design by using a combination of two or more techniques. Familiarity with all these approaches will help you both in analyzing existing tessellations and in creating new designs of your own.

Chapter 6

INVESTIGATIONS & APPLICATIONS

In this chapter we will investigate several special types of tessellations. Some types are discussed for their historical significance and beauty, while others suggest topics that you might explore recreationally or activities that you can used to develop skill in designing tessellating patterns. Our treatment of these topics is brief, and we pose some open-ended questions. The bibliography offers a listing of resources for those who are interested in studying any particular type of tessellation design in more depth.

Polyominoes, Polyiamonds, and Polyhexes

Polyominoes are shapes formed by combining two or more congruent squares along their edges. The unit squares that create the overall shape must coincide completely at an edge; sharing only a vertex is not sufficient. *Polyiamonds* are similarly created with combinations of congruent equilateral triangles; *polyhexes* are shapes created with congruent regular hexagons. Examples of these shapes are shown in figures 6-1, 6-2, and 6-3.

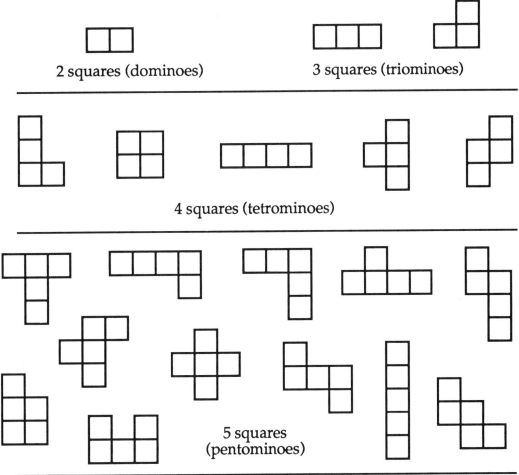

2 squares (dominoes)

3 squares (triominoes)

4 squares (tetrominoes)

5 squares
(pentominoes)

Fig. 6-1. All possible configurations of dominoes, triominoes, tetrominoes, and pentominoes (categories of polyominoes)

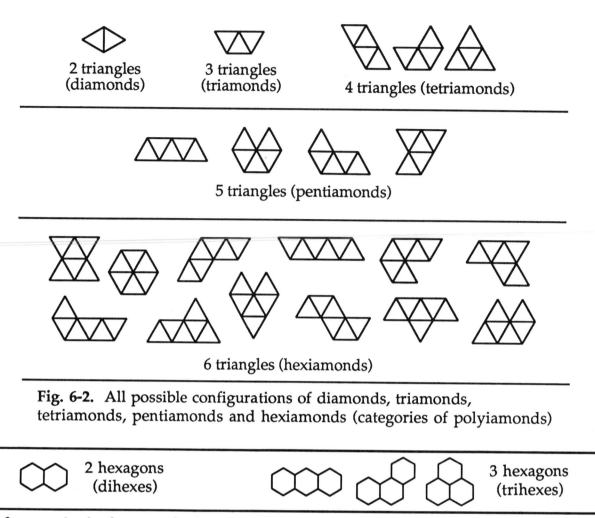

Fig. 6-2. All possible configurations of diamonds, triamonds, tetriamonds, pentiamonds and hexiamonds (categories of polyiamonds)

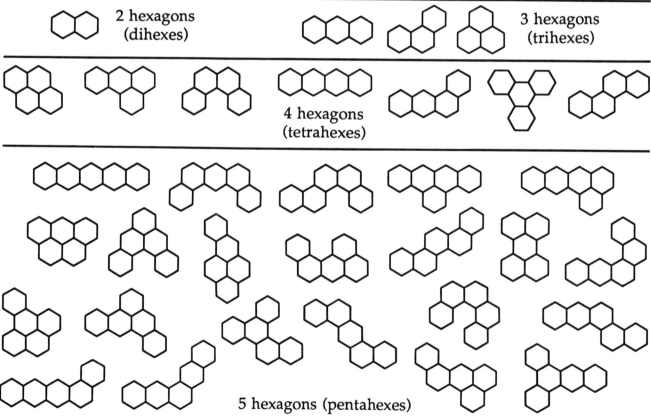

Fig. 6-3. All possible configurations of dihexes, trihexes, tetrahexes, and pentahexes (categories of polyhexes)

We can explore polyominoes, polyiamonds, and polyhexes to discover which of these special shapes tessellate. For example, we might ask ourselves, which of the pentominoes tessellate the plane? We start by looking at the twelve pentomino shapes in figure 6-4. To clarify the shapes, we have deleted adjacent sides of the five squares comprising each one, leaving only the perimeter.

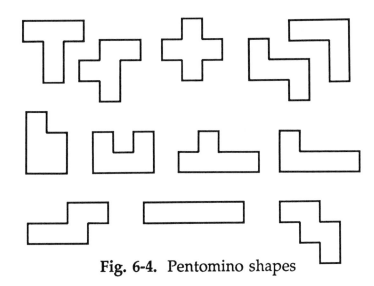

Fig. 6-4. Pentomino shapes

Figure 6-5 shows four of the pentominoes that do tessellate. Which others will tessellate?

Fig. 6-5. Examples of pentominoes tessellating

Figure 6-6 shows the twelve hexiamond shapes, and figure 6-7 shows four examples of hexiamond shapes that tessellate. Will *all* the hexiamond shapes tessellate?

Fig. 6-6. Hexiamond shapes

Fig. 6-7. Examples of hexiamonds tessellating

Figure 6-8 shows the 22 pentahex shapes. Figure 6-9 shows four examples of pentahex shapes that tessellate. Which other pentahexes will tessellate?

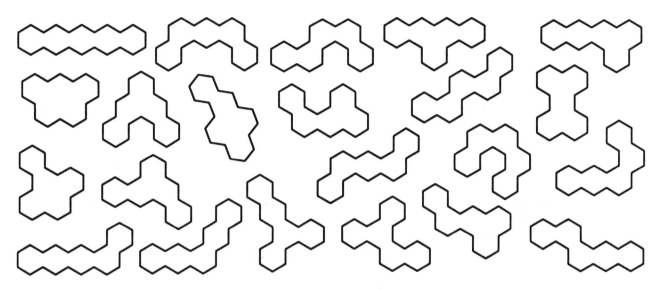

Fig. 6-8. Pentahex shapes

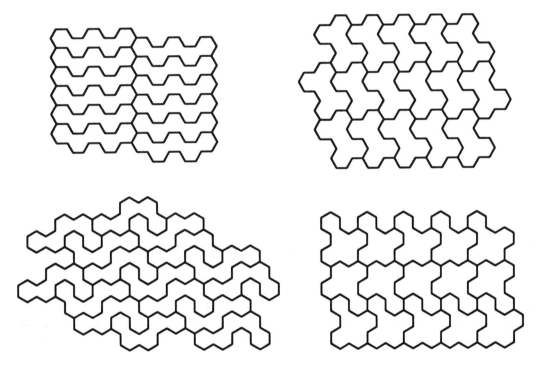

Fig. 6-9. Examples of pentahexes tessellating

As you can see, combinations of squares, equilateral triangles, and regular hexagons provide many combinations of shapes with which to explore tessellation possibilities.

Another set of shapes that we can use to explore tessellation patterns is letters of the alphabet. Letter shapes are easily sketched on dot paper. Although not all letters conveniently form block letters on a grid, especially letters containing curves, letter styles do differ considerably and we can take some artistic license in modifying a

Fig. 6-10. Tessellations with the letter T

letter shape to fit a grid. For example, figure 6-10 shows several tessellating patterns with the letter T. In this particular style, the stem of the T is quite short in relation to the crossbar. If we extend the length of the stem, we can create different tessellating T patterns as shown in figure 6-11. In both of these figures, note how we use color as one element of the tessellation pattern.

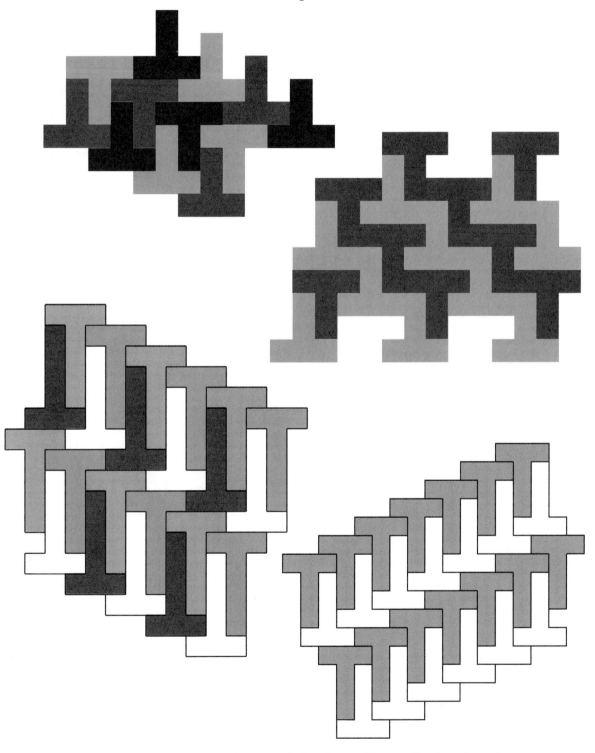

Fig. 6-11. Different shapes of the letter T tessellating the plane

While exploring with letters on dot paper or graph paper, we can experiment with color symmetries as well as with variations in the position of the tessellating shapes.

Fig. 6-12. Examples of tessellating letter shapes

Star polygons are featured in many types of ornamentation and pattern designs. They have been used as design elements by all cultures and in all periods of history. The great mathematician and astronomer Johann Kepler was one of the first to explore the tessellating properties of regular polygons and regular star polygons. His book *Harmonice Mundi* (1619) contains remarkable examples of tilings with these star shapes.

We might define regular star polygons as non-convex polygons, all of whose sides are congruent, containing two angles of different sizes, one convex and one concave. A star polygon can be created by drawing congruent isosceles triangles as star points off the sides of a regular polygon. Figure 6-13 shows a variety of star polygons formed this way; the original regular polygon is indicated by dotted lines.

Fig. 6-13. Examples of star polygons

We could also construct a star polygon by (a) dividing a circle into a given number of equal arcs, (b) connecting the endpoints of the arcs in some pattern (other than consecutively), and (c) eliminating certain line segments to create the final star polygon. The next several figures demonstrate this procedure.

Figure 6-14(a) shows a circle that we have divided into eight equal 45° arcs; figure 6-14(b) shows how we connect the endpoints of every other arc; figure 6-14(c) shows the final star polygon after we have eliminated the superfluous line segments. Since the star is formed from eight points by segments that join every second point, we call this shape a *2/8 star polygon*.

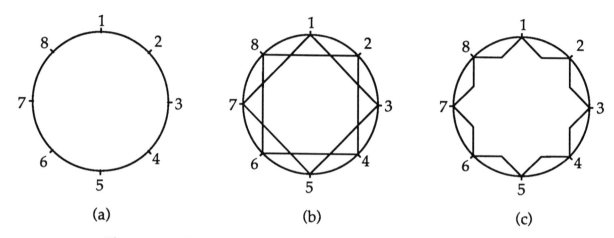

Fig. 6-14. Three stages of construction of a 2/8 star polygon

If we chose to join every *third* point on the circle divided into eight equal arcs, and if we followed the same procedures as in figure 6-14, then we would form the 3/8 star polygon (figure 6-15). Compare the 2/8 and 3/8 figures; what are the differences?

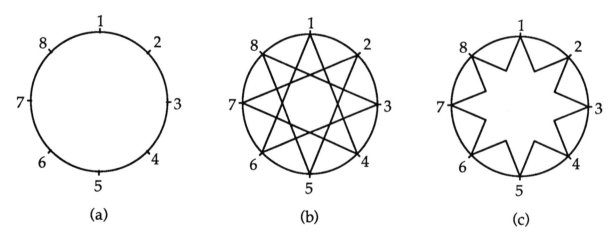

Fig. 6-15. Three stages of construction of a 3/8 star polygon

We can derive a four-pointed star from the 3/8 star by omitting part of it, as shown in figure 6-16. As you can see, a circle divided into eight equal arcs can be the basis for several different types of regular star polygons.

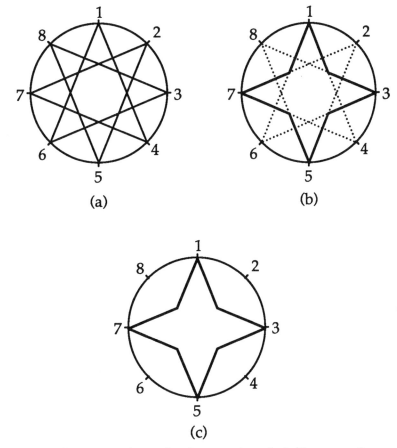

(a)

(b)

(c)

Fig. 6-16. Construction of a four-pointed, 3/8 star polygon

Figures 6-17 through 6-21 show the construction of star polygons by the same basic procedure, starting with a circle divided variously into five, ten, and sixteen equal arcs.

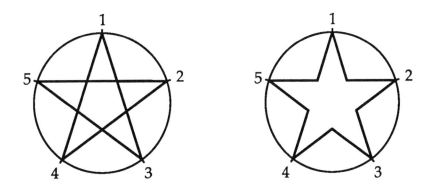

Fig. 6-17. Construction of a 2/5 star polygon

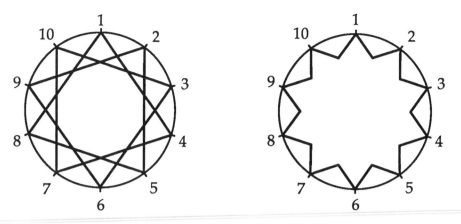

Fig. 6-18. Construction of a 3/10 star polygon

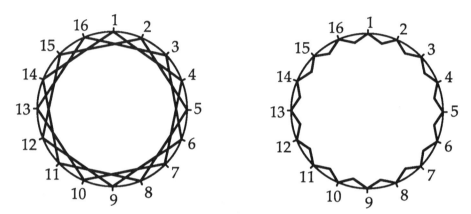

Fig. 6-19. Construction of a 3/16 star polygon

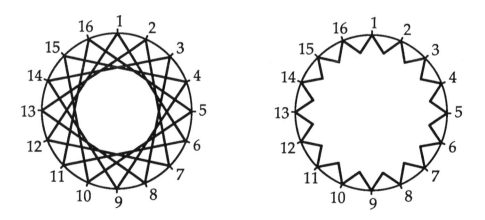

Fig. 6-20. Construction of a 5/16 star polygon

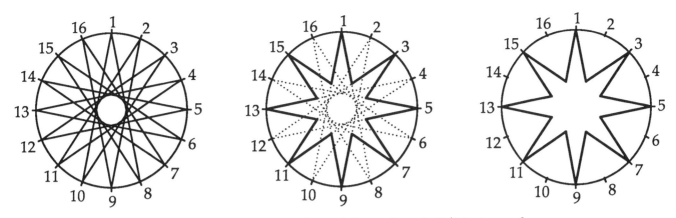

Fig. 6-21. Construction of an eight-pointed, 7/16 star polygon

Another technique for constructing regular star polygons is to choose the size of the acute angle and draw the resulting star. For example, suppose we want to create a five-pointed star polygon whose acute interior angles are each 20 degrees. In order to construct this star, we also need to determine the size of its interior reflex angles. This is easily done. A five-pointed star is a decagon. In chapter 3 (page 51) we saw that all decagons contain 1440° in the sum of their ten interior angles. If each acute angle of our star measures 20°, there will be a total of 100° in the five acute angles. This leaves 1340° for the other five angles, and 1340°/5 equals 268°. Thus, each of the interior reflex angles will measure 268°. We can now construct our star polygon using a straightedge and a protractor (or, if available, a personal computer). The three stages of construction are shown in figure 6-22: (a) draw a 20° angle; (b) add congruent adjacent edges to form 268° angles; and (c) continue the drawing to complete the star polygon. Note that we can choose any convenient length for the measure of the edges and need only be sure that each edge is the same length.

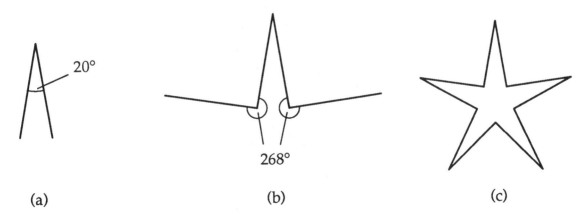

     (a)   (b)   (c)

Fig. 6-22. Star polygon constructed with 20° angles

We can create an infinite number of five-pointed star polygons of different shapes by first selecting an angle size. Figure 6-23 shows just a few examples.

Fig. 6-23. Five-pointed star polygons with acute angles measuring 30°, 40°, 50°, 60°, and 70°

Now that we've learned several ways of constructing star polygons, let's consider how we might use them as elements in tessellating patterns. Star polygons do not tessellate by themselves but will often tessellate in combination with other regular polygons. The star polygon in figure 6-24 joins with three congruent stars to create an additional shape—a square—with sides the same length as the edges of the star. This combination of shapes tessellates as shown in figure 6-25.

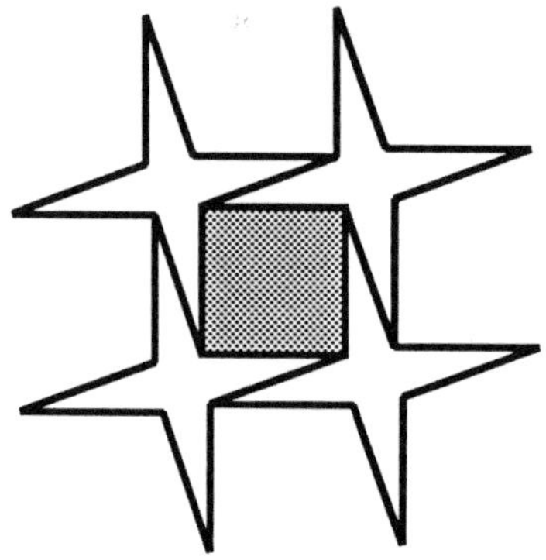

Fig. 6-24. Star polygons and a square

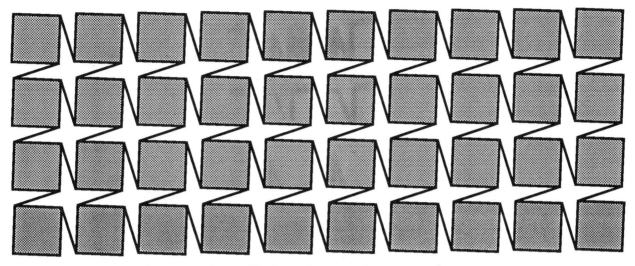

Fig. 6-25. Tessellation of star polygons and squares

Imagine, in figure 6-25, that the shaded squares are all joined at their vertices by rigid rods (the edges of the stars) that will not bend but will pivot where they are connected to the squares. Now try to visualize that by pulling the squares farther apart, we move all the squares and also enlarge the star polygons. In the process, each of the acute interior angles of the star increases in size. The resulting change produces a tessellation like that in figure 6-26.

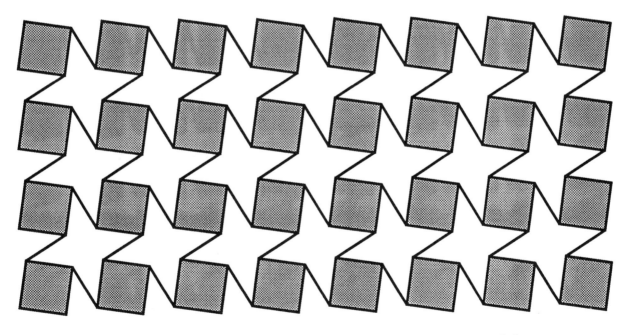

Fig. 6-26. Tessellation similar to figure 6-25, using squares of the same size and star polygons with edges of the same length but different interior angles

This "pulling apart" process is further demonstrated in figures 6-27 through 6-34, where we see how the various tessellations of star polygons and squares make a transition from a pattern of tessellating squares of one size to a different pattern of tessellating squares of two sizes. Note that any angle less than 90° can be used for the acute angle of the star polygon.

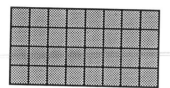

Fig. 6-27. Tessellating squares

Fig. 6-28. Star polygons (10°)

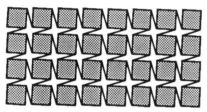

Fig. 6-29. Star polygons (20°)

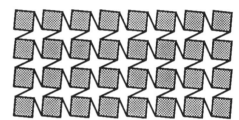

Fig. 6-30. Star polygons (30°)

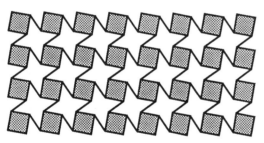

Fig. 6-31. Star polygons (45°)

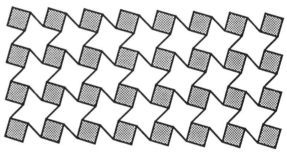

Fig. 6-32. Star polygons (60°)

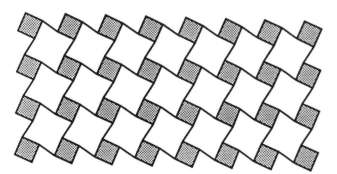

Fig. 6-33. Star polygons (80°)

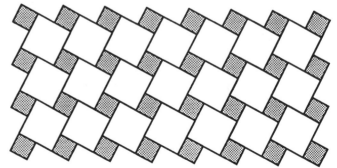

Fig. 6-34. Tessellating squares (90°)

Similarly, we can "pull apart" a tessellation of equilateral triangles to create patterns with star polygons, each triangle having the same edge length as the star polygons. The following series of figures shows that as the star polygon's acute angles grow larger, the stars approach a point where they become larger equilateral triangles (with 60° angles).

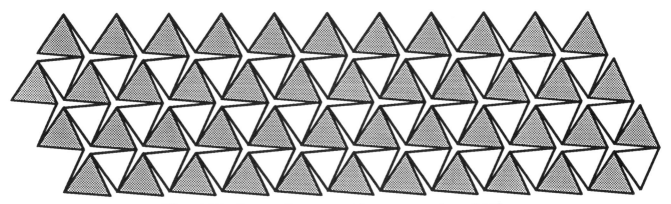

Fig. 6-35. Star polygons with acute angles of 10°

Fig. 6-36. Star polygons with acute angles of 25°

Fig. 6-37. Star polygons with acute angles of 50°

We can also create tessellations by combining hexagons with star polygons, as seen in figures 6-38 and 6-39. It would be interesting to explore whether or not *any* regular polygon could be similarly combined with star polygons to create a tessellating pattern. If you want to pursue this, you might start by tracing the regular polygons on page 45 or page 71.

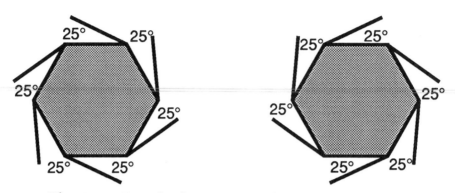

Fig. 6-38. Regular hexagons with sides rotated 25°

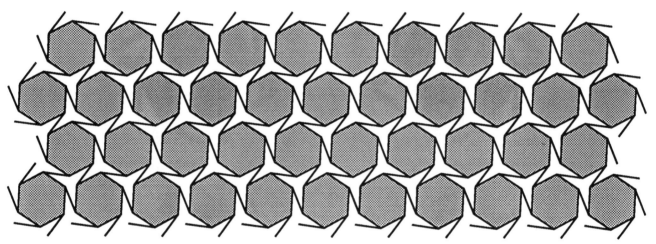

Fig. 6-39. Tessellation of star polygons and hexagons

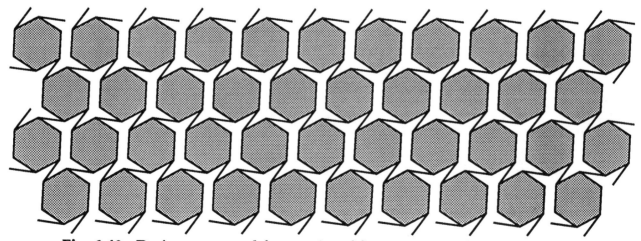

Fig. 6-40. Design generated from units of figure 6-38, with new shapes (equilateral polygons) that are neither star polygons nor regular polygons

Designs containing star polygons can be modified into new designs through some of the techniques presented in chapter 5. For example, figure 6-40 shows the design we make from figure 6-39 when we combine two of the three-pointed star polygons into a single new shape. Alternatively, can you visualize what design we might create by inscribing six-pointed star polygons in the hexagons, then deleting the lines of the hexagons?

Many unique design discoveries result from experimentation with existing designs. Such experiments can increase our understanding of the relationships between fundamental shapes such as regular polygons and star polygons and may give us even more ideas. Figures 6-41 through 6-55 demonstrate some experimental designs; try to visualize a modification of each one.

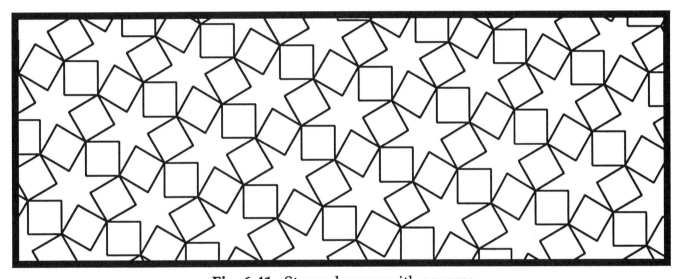

Fig. 6-41. Star polygons with squares

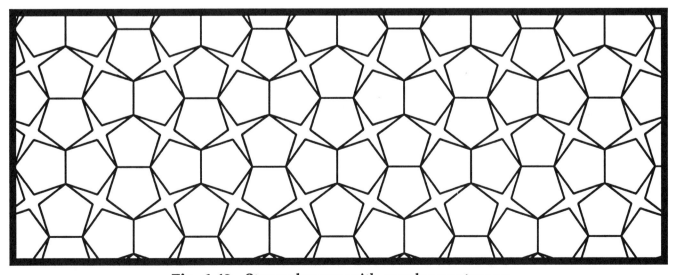

Fig. 6-42. Star polygons with regular pentagons

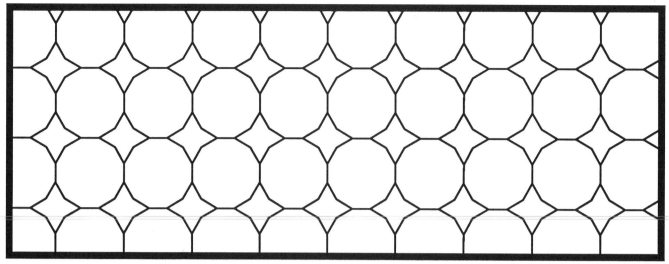

Fig. 6-43. Star polygons with regular dodecagons

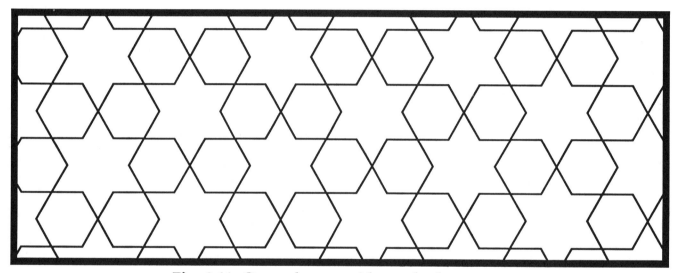

Fig. 6-44. Star polygons with regular hexagons

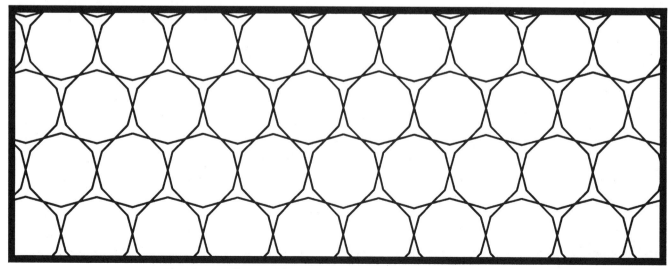

Fig. 6-45. Star polygons with regular dodecagons

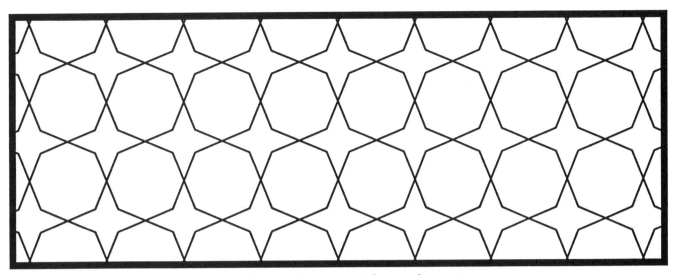

Fig. 6-46. Star polygons with regular octagons

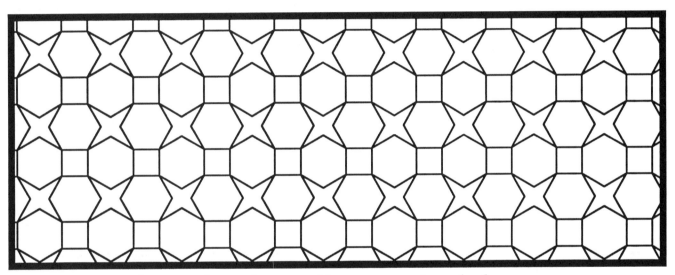

Fig. 6-47. Star polygons with squares and regular hexagons

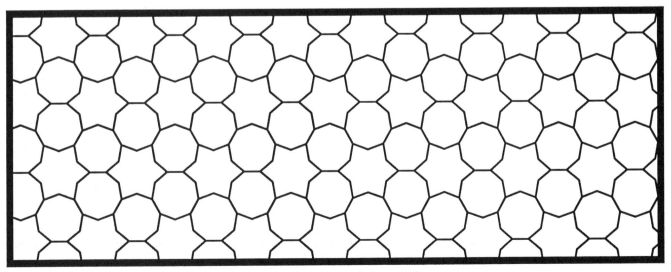

Fig. 6-48. Star polygons with regular nonagons

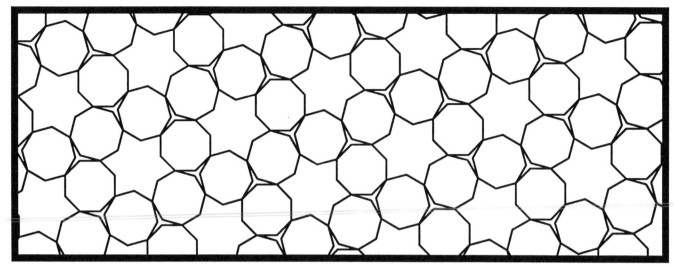

Fig. 6-49. Two types of star polygons with regular octagons

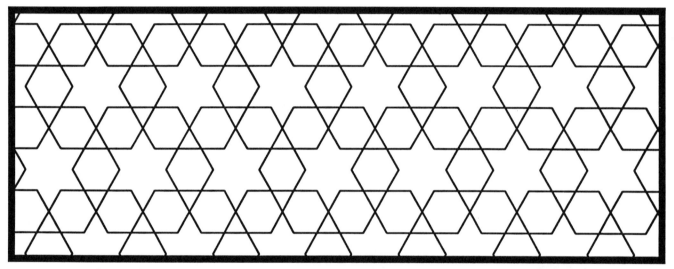

Fig. 6-50. Star polygons with equilateral triangles and regular hexagons

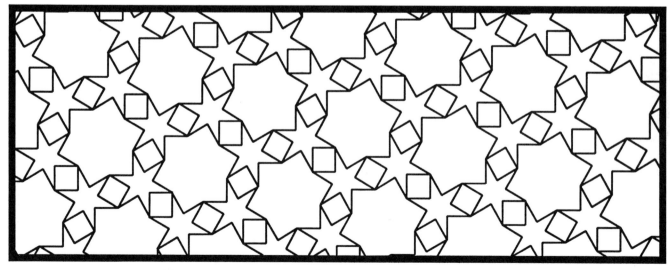

Fig. 6-51. Two types of star polygons with squares

Fig. 6-52. Star polygons with equilateral triangles and squares

Fig. 6-53. Star polygons, equilateral triangles, squares, and regular hexagons

Fig. 6-54. Star polygons, equilateral triangles, squares, and regular octagons

Fig. 6-55. Two types of star polygons with equilateral triangles

Islamic Designs

More than any other culture, Islam developed the art of geometric pattern. The early religious leaders of Islam interpreted Muhammad's preaching against idolatry as an injunction against the representation of humans or animals in art. Consequently, for centuries, Islamic art consisted of three types: designs derived from plant life, calligraphy, and repeating geometric shapes.

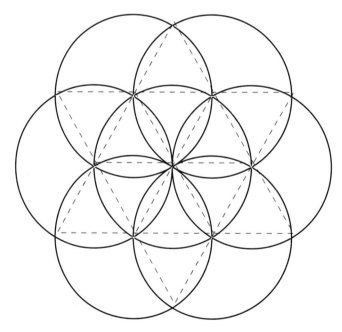

Fig. 6-56. Congruent intersecting circles form a triangular grid.

All Islamic designs were constructed with compass and straightedge only, so the circle became the basis for their geometric designs. Circles defined triangular, square, or hexagonal grids upon which the designs were constructed. These are the same grids we know as the three regular tessellations. Figures 6-56 through 6-60 demonstrate the fundamental relationships of congruent circles intersecting to form the basic grids.

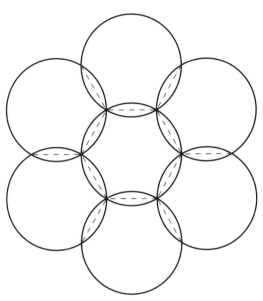

Fig. 6-57. Congruent circles intersect at one-sixth arc positions, forming a hexagonal grid.

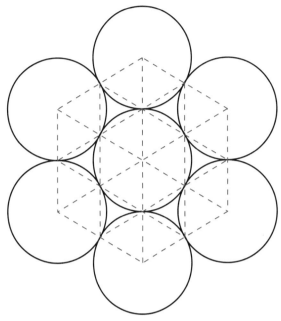

Fig. 6-58. Tangent congruent circles form a triangular grid.

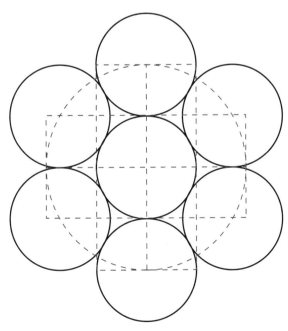

Fig. 6-59. Tangent lines form a square grid.

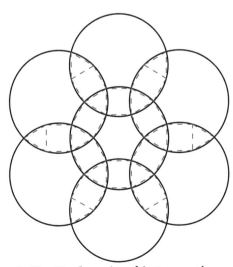

Fig. 6-60. Each pair of intersecting circles cuts quarter-circles, creating a semiregular tessellation.

Many Islamic designs reveal the semiregular tessellation patterns described in chapter 3. On the following pages, we show but a few of the simpler and more popular Islamic designs. A visual analysis will reveal many of the concepts and techniques discussed in earlier chapters. Notice the extensive use of star polygons throughout.

Fig. 6-61. Star polygons on a triangular grid

Fig. 6-62. Star polygons further separated on the grid

Figures 6-61 and 6-62 show two design ideas starting with six-pointed star polygons on a triangular grid. Working with the arrangement shown in figure 6-62, we can divide the space between the stars symmetrically (figures 6-63 and 6-64) to create a common Islamic design (figure 6-65).

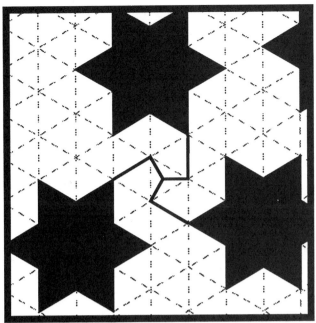

Fig. 6-63. White area between stars is divided symmetrically from the center.

Fig. 6-64. Dividing each white area creates a uniform angular S shape.

Fig. 6-65. Completed Islamic design

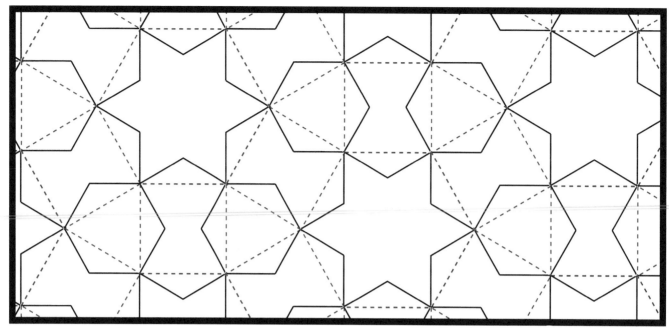

Fig. 6-66. Underlying grid pattern of the design in figure 6-67 is a semiregular tessellation.

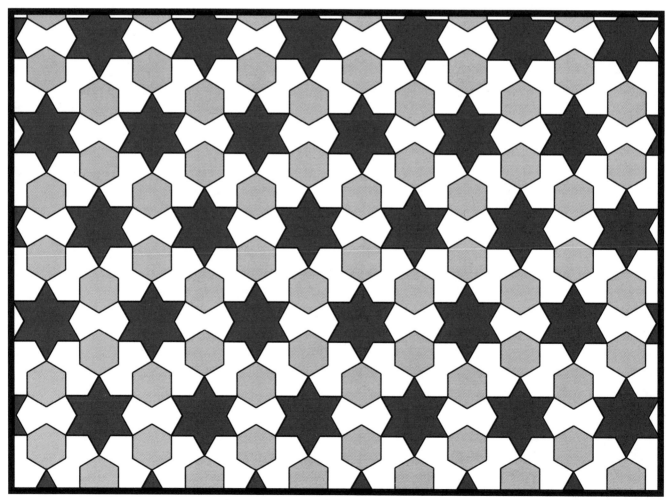

Fig. 6-67. Popular Islamic pattern

Fig. 6-68. Pattern from figure 6-67 extended to three dimensions

Fig. 6-69. Islamic design with eight-pointed stars

Fig. 6-70. Islamic design with star polygons and interlocking hexagons

Fig. 6-71. Islamic design with two types of star polygons

Fig. 6-72. Islamic design with regular and nonregular star polygons

Chapter 7

CREATING
ESCHER-LIKE
TESSELLATIONS

The late Dutch graphic artist Maurits Cornelis Escher was the creator of many artistic and perplexing tessellations whose repetitive patterns appear, at first glance, to be beyond the grasp of artist, mathematician, and layman alike. As we will discover in this chapter, he was experimenting with some of the same geometric principles we have touched on in our investigations, and he created his tessellations using some of the same techniques we explored in chapter 5.

Escher was born in the Netherlands in 1898. His first work was strictly representational, yet his landscapes reveal a fascination with the intricate structure he saw in nature and architecture. Escher's preoccupation with tessellations developed after a repeat trip to Spain in 1936, where he visited a structure that had first intrigued him in 1922—the Alhambra. The walls, floors, and ceilings of this 13th-century palace-fortress, built by the Moors, are covered with mosaics of great variety and beauty. Escher spent days copying the patterns in his notebook and remarked, "This is the richest source of inspiration that I have ever struck. . . . What a pity it is that the religion of the Moors forbade them to make graven images!"

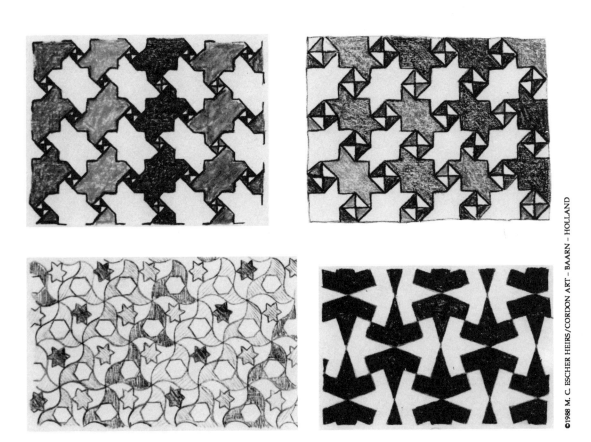

Fig. 7-1. Sketches made by Escher at the Alhambra

Although inspired by the Moorish mosaics, Escher did not restrict himself to abstract geometrical designs. In fact, he did the opposite—he restricted himself to *animate* forms as he explored the world of tessellations. With extraordinary inventiveness, he created tessellating shapes that resembled birds, fish, lizards, dogs, humans, butterflies, and the occasional creature of his own invention. He left notebooks filled with studies and sketches of repeating patterns, many of which he incorporated into woodcuts and lithographs. One such lithograph, *Reptiles* (figure 7-2), shows an intrepid lizard crawling out of Escher's two-dimensional sketch to explore the real world before rejoining his fellow reptiles in the interlocking design.

Fig. 7-2. *Reptiles*, M. C. Escher

If you study the notebook drawing in the lithograph, you will notice a grid of regular hexagons superimposed on it. Even though the reptiles are turning this way and that, each fits in a hexagon in exactly the same way—a relationship that you can see more clearly in figure 7-3.

Fig. 7-3. A grid of hexagons underlying the reptile tessellation

This reptilian creature appears to have "evolved" from a regular hexagon. We will discover in this chapter that, in fact, each of Escher's tessellating creatures was based on a polygon that he modified by certain procedures to create a distinctive contour.

Until his death in 1972, Escher maintained his interest in tessellations, returning again and again to what he once called "the mental gymnastics of my puzzles." In this chapter we will analyze several of Escher's tessellations, each formed by a single tessellating shape, and discover how we can create similar patterns ourselves.

Modifying Polygons by Translation

In 1960 Escher was commissioned to design a tiled façade for a school in The Hague. He created a motif consisting of two elements, a light-colored Pegasus and a darker one. The two winged horses are, apart from their color, exactly the same, both in contour and in orientation.

Fig. 7-4. *Pegasus*, M. C. Escher

Suppose we had a transparent duplicate or tracing of the Pegasus tessellation shown in figure 7-4. If we placed this tracing on top of the original, we could translate (slide) it horizontally until one horse ended up exactly on top of an adjacent horse—thus bringing the design into coincidence with itself (ignoring the change in coloring). We could do the same thing vertically.

By actual measurement, we would find that the magnitude of the horizontal translation just described is exactly equal to that of the vertical translation. This suggests that a square is somehow involved in the design of the tessellating shape. Indeed, we find that the tessellation fits neatly into a grid of squares (figure 7-5), with horizontal and vertical lines intersecting at the tip of each horse's lower jaw. (There are other possible placements for the vertices of the square grid, but using the tip of the lower jaw works nicely because we end up with the major part of the horse's body in a single square.) Note that each horse fits in its square in exactly the same way as its fellow horses.

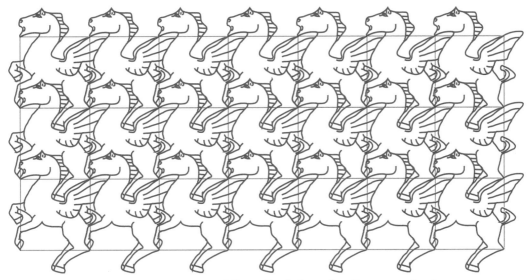

Fig. 7-5. A square grid underlying the *Pegasus* design

Let's investigate how we might create this shape by modifying a square by translation—a technique discussed in chapter 5. The process is shown in figure 7-6. As we analyze the various transformations in this chapter, we will always number the sides of the original polygon clockwise and refer to each side by number. Thus, we number from 1 to 4 the sides of a square in which a horse is inscribed. Studying the horse's contour, we see that we might first modify side 1 and translate this modification to side 3. Protrusions (or bumps) on side 1 become congruent indentations (or holes) on side 3, and vice versa. In like manner, we make a modification to side 2 and translate it to side 4. Despite these changes, the modified square has the same area as the original or *parent* square.

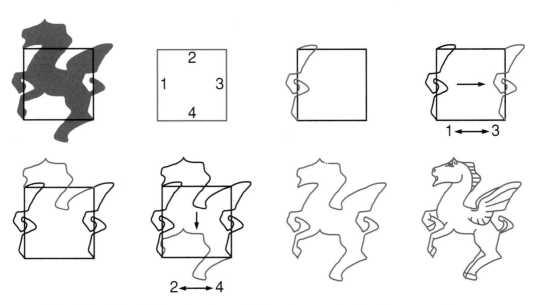

Fig. 7-6. Modifying by translation to create the Pegasus shape

We can now try this same procedure to create our own Escher-like tessellating shape. There are two ways to approach our modification of a polygon to create a non-polygonal tessellating shape. One way is to have some specific object in mind—such as a horse—and to modify the sides of the polygon until its contour resembles that object. A second approach is to modify the sides of the polygon with random curves, then interpret the resulting shape by adding details to highlight its interior.

In figure 7-7, we see a square that has been modified by translation (with no specific object in mind). Figure 7-8 shows the modified square interpreted first as a witch and then, with the shape rotated counterclockwise 90°, as a winged seahorse.

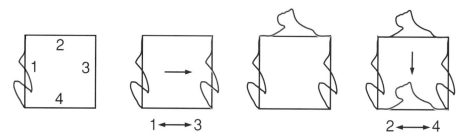

Fig. 7-7. Modifying by translation

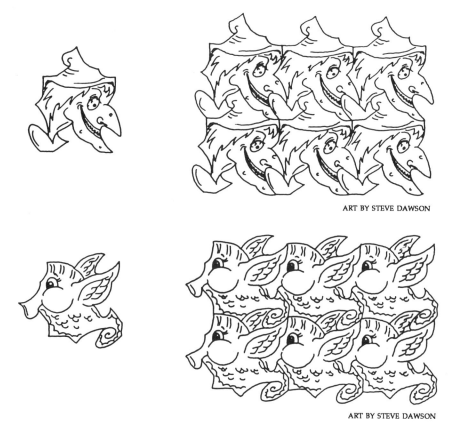

ART BY STEVE DAWSON

ART BY STEVE DAWSON

Fig. 7-8. Alternative interpretations of the same tessellating shape

Each of the tessellating shapes in figure 7-9 was similarly created by modifying a square by translation. In the first instance, the artist had a dog in mind and modified the square until its contour resembled that object. In the second instance, the artist made random modifications and interpreted the shape after the fact, adding details to represent a woman.

Fig. 7-9. Two more tessellations created by modifying a square by translation

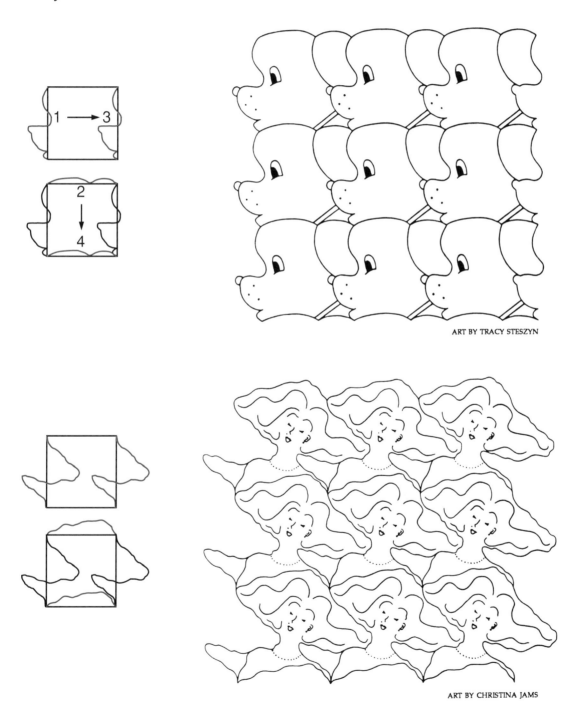

ART BY TRACY STESZYN

ART BY CHRISTINA JAMS

Any quadrilateral having parallel and congruent sides can be modified by translating the modification of one side to the opposite side. Figure 7-10 demonstrates the result when we modify a rectangle and a parallelogram in this way. Adding details to the interior of each shape gives us the two tessellations shown below.

Fig. 7-10. Tessellations created by modifying a rectangle and a parallelogram by translation

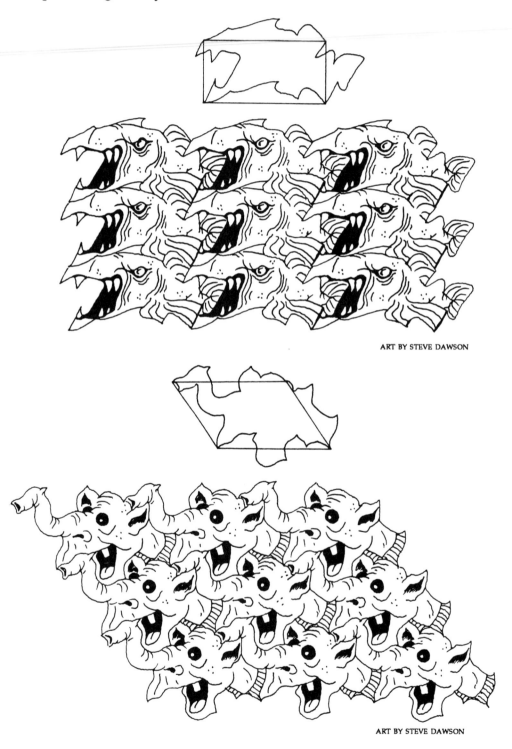

ART BY STEVE DAWSON

ART BY STEVE DAWSON

We can extend this method to include regular hexagons or, more generally, any hexagon having parallel and congruent sides. (Recall that in chapter 2, we discovered that any hexagon whose opposite sides are parallel and congruent will tessellate.) In hexagonal tessellations we have *three* sets of opposite sides to be modified. The resulting non-polygonal shape has the same area and tessellates the plane in the same manner as its parent hexagon. The tessellation, with details added, is shown in figure 7-12.

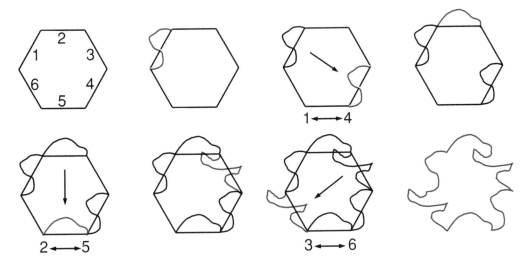

Fig. 7-11. A modification of a regular hexagon

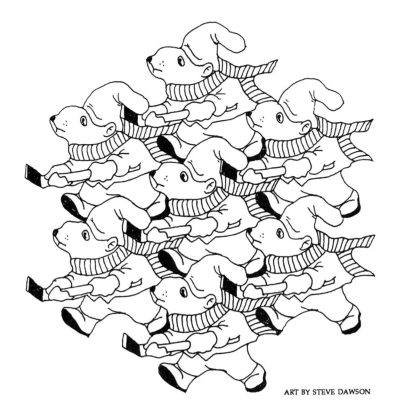

ART BY STEVE DAWSON

Fig. 7-12. Tessellation based on a hexagon modified by translation

The Escher tessellation of fish shown in figure 7-13, like the Pegasus tessellation, consists of identical animals, light and dark. However, the two types of fish are oriented differently, the dark fish swimming to the right and the light ones to the left.

Fig. 7-13. *Fish*, M. C. Escher

This tessellation has translational symmetry (as do all the Escher and Escher-like tessellations in this chapter). Thus we can bring the design into coincidence with itself by translating it either horizontally or vertically until adjacent light fish or dark fish coincide.

The tessellation also has rotational symmetry. That is, a light and a dark fish can exchange places if we rotate them 180° about a point between their left eyes. (You might trace a fish onto a sheet of translucent paper or acetate and verify this for yourself.) If we rotate the figure in this way two times, it will return to its original position; thus we say that the tessellation has two-fold rotational symmetry.

There are actually four different centers of two-fold rotation that will allow a light and a dark fish to exchange places. Each is the midpoint of a side of a scalene quadrilateral. Figure 7-14 shows the grid formed by these scalene quadrilaterals. Note that they are not parallelograms; we know this is not a problem since all quadrilaterals tessellate.

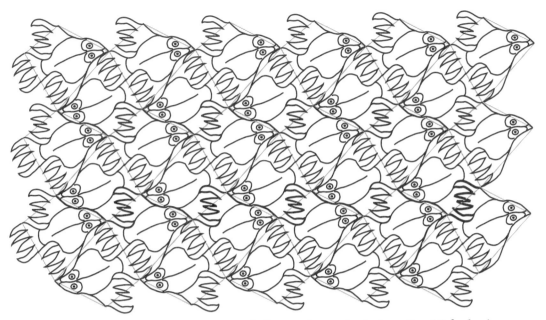

Fig. 7-14. A grid of scalene quadrilaterals underlying the *Fish* design

Note that although the orientation of the quadrilaterals alternates, each fish fits in its quadrilateral in exactly the same way as all the others. Let's investigate how we might create this fish shape from the original quadrilateral (see figure 7-15). We number the sides of that quadrilateral and study the contour of the fish inside it. Looking at each side separately, we see a type of change familiar from chapter 5: modifying by rotation about the midpoint of a side. That is, we modify a half-side of side 1 and rotate our modification 180° about the midpoint of that side. As a result, a hole on half of side 1 becomes a congruent bump on the other half. As you can see in figure 7-15, the same is true of all four sides.

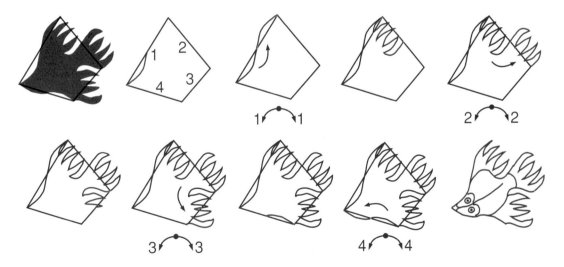

Fig. 7-15. Modifying by rotation about midpoints of sides

Any quadrilateral will tessellate if we rotate it 180° about the midpoint of each of its sides. The four angles of the quadrilateral, totalling 360°, then surround each vertex in the tessellation, as shown in figure 7-16.

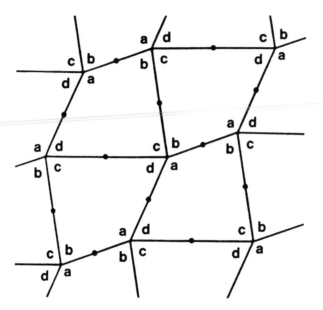

Fig. 7-16. The orientation of a quadrilateral in its tessellation

Given the enormous variety of quadrilaterals available to us, we can use rotation about midpoints of sides to create a wealth of Escher-like tessellating shapes. Each resulting tessellation will have four different centers of two-fold rotation: the midpoints of the four sides of each tessellating shape. Figures 7-17 through 7-21 demonstrate some of the possibilities.

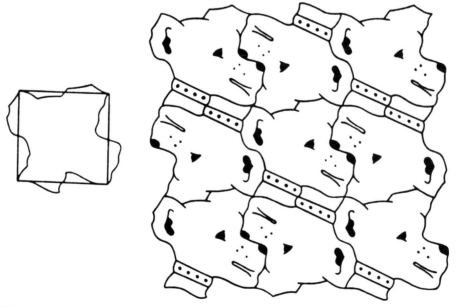

Fig. 7-17. A square modified by rotation about midpoints of sides

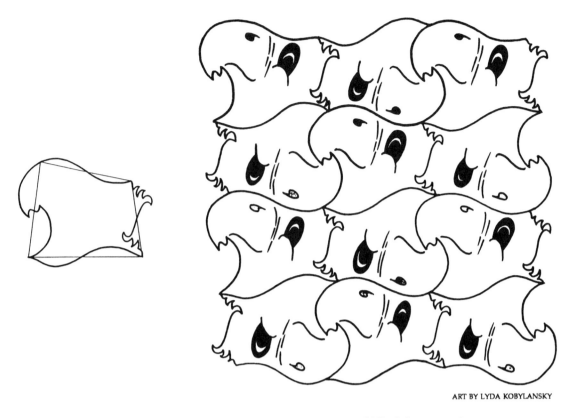

Fig. 7-18. A scalene quadrilateral modified by rotation about midpoints of sides

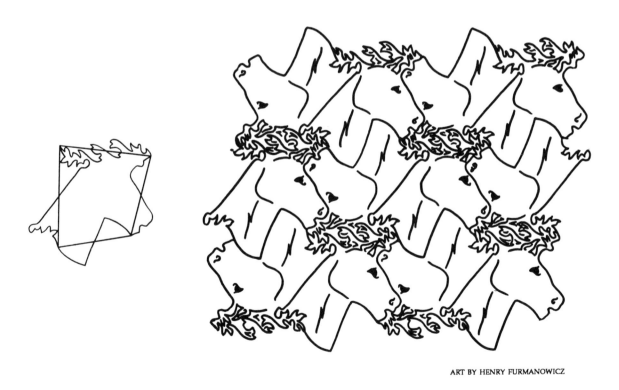

Fig. 7-19. A scalene quadrilateral modified by rotation about midpoints of sides

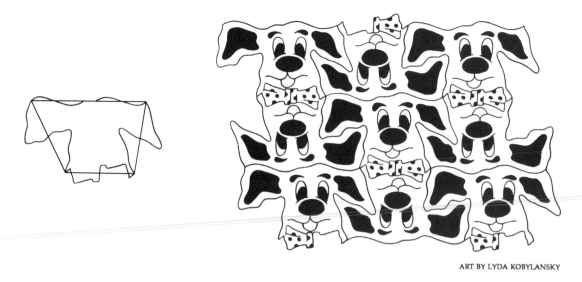

Fig. 7-20. A trapezoid modified by rotation about midpoints of sides

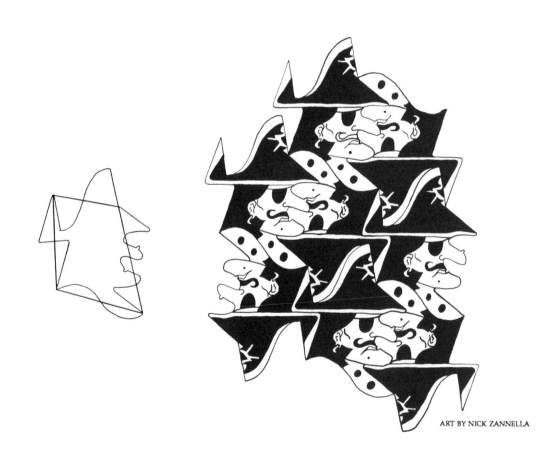

Fig. 7-21. A scalene quadrilateral modified by rotation about midpoints of sides

As we saw in chapter 5, we can use this procedure with any triangle as well. Figure 7-22 shows two examples of tessellating shapes created by modifying each half-side of a triangle and rotating the modification 180° about the midpoint of the side. See if you can find three different centers of two-fold rotation in each design.

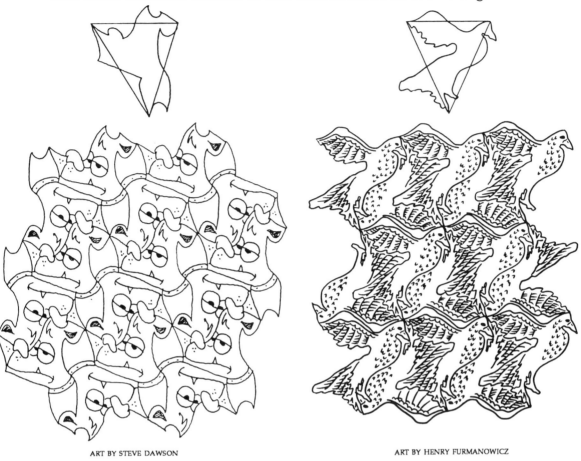

ART BY STEVE DAWSON   ART BY HENRY FURMANOWICZ

Fig. 7-22. Triangles modified by rotation about midpoints of sides

Modifying by rotation about midpoints of sides *cannot* be used to modify tessellating hexagons, as we discovered in chapter 5 (page 140). However, there is one exception. If we make exactly the same half-side modification to all six sides of a regular hexagon, so that the figure has six-fold rotational symmetry about its center, then the new shape will tessellate. (In fact, the generating polygon is an equilateral triangle, one-sixth of the hexagon.)

Fig. 7-23. Modifying all six sides of a regular hexagon the same way produces a tessellating shape.

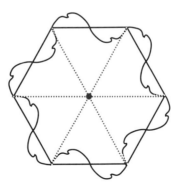

©1988 M. C. ESCHER HEIRS/CORDON ART – BAARN – HOLLAND

Fig. 7-24. *Lizard I*, M. C. Escher

Now let's consider a somewhat more complex design, the Escher tessellation of lizards shown in figure 7-24. Like the Pegasus and fish designs, this tessellation has translational symmetry. That is, a lizard of either color can be made to coincide with a lizard of the same or opposite color by a simple translation in some direction. This tessellation also has rotational symmetry.

Note that as we look for symmetries, we are seeking an underlying grid of polygons—as we did with the Pegasus and fish tessellations. Once we determine the polygonal shape on which the lizard is based, we should be able to discover a procedure for creating the tessellating shape. In tessellations with rotational symmetry, the vertices of the polygons in the underlying grid are usually rotation points. Thus, as we analyze Escher tessellations, we will always look for rotation points.

In this tessellation, each lizard's right "elbow," the extreme tip of its right leg, its left knee, and the extreme tip of its left "arm" are points of two-fold rotational symmetry. That is, each lizard can be made to coincide with an adjacent lizard of the *same* color by a 180° turn about any of these points. Note that these four points mark the vertices of a parallelogram.

Fig. 7-25. A grid of parallelograms underlying the *Lizard I* design

Figure 7-25 shows, then, the underlying structure of this tessellation—a grid of parallelograms. If we study the contour of a lizard inscribed in a parallelogram, we find that we can create this shape by a procedure that *combines* translation and rotation about midpoints of sides (figure 7-26). First, a modification to side 2 is translated to side 4. Then, modifications to half of side 1 and side 3 are rotated 180° about the midpoints of those same sides. Note that in the tessellation, adjacent lizards of opposite color can be made to coincide by two-fold rotation about both of these midpoints.

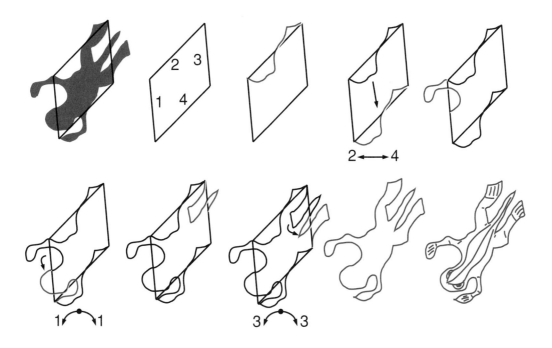

Fig. 7-26. Modifying by translation *and* midpoint rotation

We can follow the same pattern—translation of sides 2 and 4, and rotation about the midpoints of sides 1 and 3—to create our own Escher-like tessellating shape, as shown in figure 7-27. Here the parallelogram we use is a rectangle. Figure 7-28 shows the modified rectangle interpreted either as a rabbit or, with the shape rotated 180°, as a bulldog with a snappy bow tie.

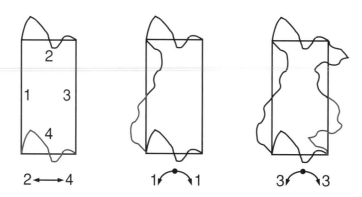

Fig. 7-27. Modifying by translation *and* midpoint rotation

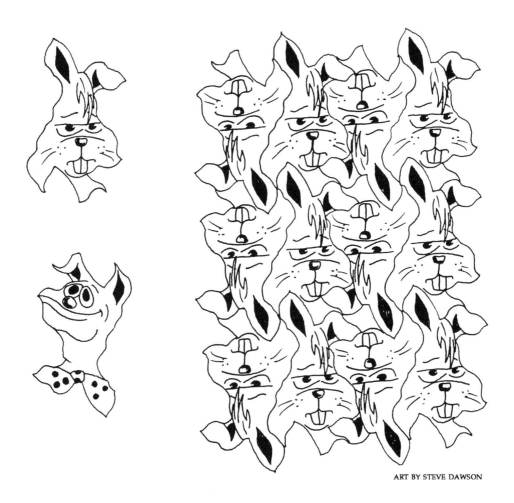

Fig. 7-28. Two interpretations of the modified rectangle

Fig. 7-29. *Lizard II*, M. C. Escher

Modifying Polygons by Rotation about Vertices

In figure 7-29 we see another Escher tessellation of lizards with both translational and rotational symmetry. As before, we will look for rotation points to locate the vertices of the underlying grid; then we will try to discover the procedure for creating the tessellating lizard shape. Concentrating first on either the white or the black lizards, we see points of two-fold rotation at their noses, at their right knees, at their right front feet, and at their left rear feet. That is, at any of those points, a rotation of 180° brings two same-color lizards into coincidence. If we look at the design as a whole, ignoring color differences, we discover that the latter two points—right front feet and left rear feet—are also centers of four-fold rotation. That is, a rotation of 90° about either point brings the lizards into coincidence. If we connect all four points with sets of perpendicular lines, we find a square grid, as shown in figure 7-30.

Fig. 7-30. A grid of squares underlying the *Lizard II* design

Let's isolate one lizard from that grid and see how it was created from a square (figure 7-31). We number the sides and, for this procedure, we also letter the vertices of a square. Studying the contour of the lizard, we find that we can modify side 1 and rotate our modification about vertex A to side 2. As a result, a bump on side 1 becomes a congruent hole on side 2, and vice versa. We do the same with the remaining sides, modifying side 3 and rotating this modification about vertex C to side 4.

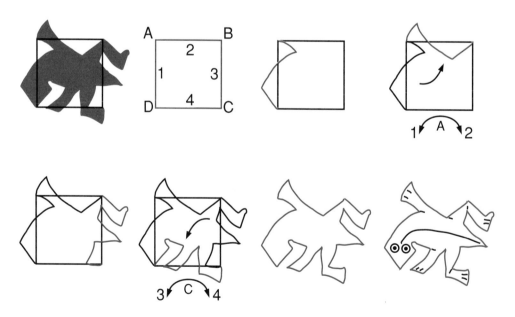

Fig. 7-31. Modifying by rotation about vertices to create the lizard shape

It is interesting to consider the orientation of the lizard shapes in the resulting tessellation. As you can see in figure 7-30, four lizards together form a larger unit that tessellates by translation alone. But within that four-lizard unit, each lizard has a different orientation. This is the first Escher design we have explored in which the shape is turned in four different directions.

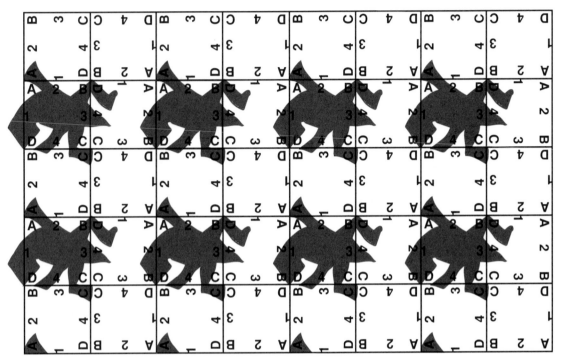

Fig. 7-32. The changing orientation of the lizards in the tessellation

Figure 7-32 shows the underlying square grid with the sides and vertices of each square labeled according to the orientation of its inscribed lizard. If you study this configuration, you will see that side 1 always touches side 2 and that side 3 always touches side 4. The letters in the diagram help point out the four-fold symmetries (around vertices A and C) and the two-fold symmetries (at vertices B and D).

The generation of this tessellation is easier than its many symmetries might suggest. Note that the red lizards appear in squares that are identically oriented. Starting with any one of these lizards, we could generate the tessellation simply by rotating the shape 90° four times about vertex C (until it returns to its original location), then translating it two squares, both horizontally and vertically, and repeating the process. Alternatively, we could start with a four-fold rotation about vertex A and follow the same steps.

Now let's try to create our own tessellating shape by modifying two opposite sides of a square and rotating each modification about a vertex to an adjacent side. This is what we have done in figure 7-33. We started with a bird in mind and modified the sides of the square until its contour resembled a bird with wings outspread. The resulting tessellation has two centers of four-fold rotation and two centers of two-fold rotation, as does the Escher tessellation whose pattern inspired it.

Fig. 7-33. Modifying by rotation about vertices

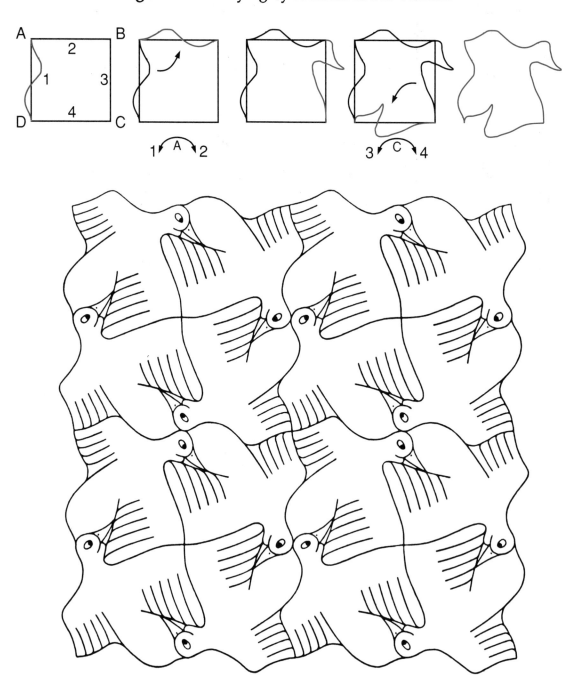

Figure 7-34 contains two more examples of tessellating shapes that result from rotating modifications about vertices. In creating each of these, the artist made random modifications to the sides of a square, then interpreted the resulting shapes as a goofy moose and a rogue in a plumed hat.

Fig. 7-34. Two further examples of modifying a square by rotation about vertices

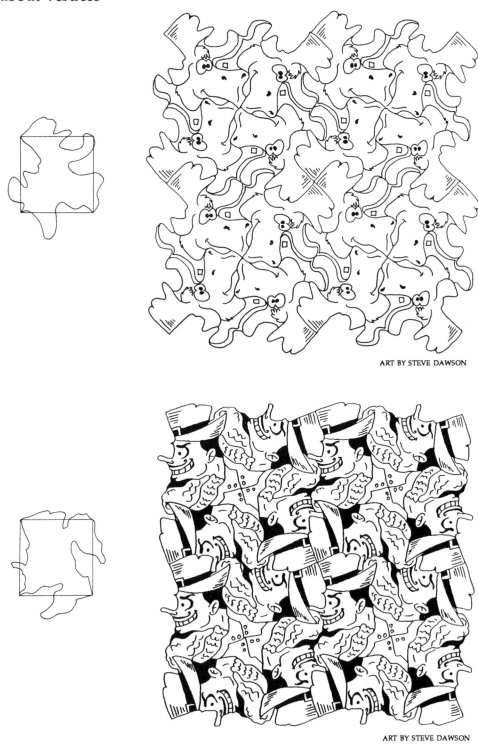

ART BY STEVE DAWSON

ART BY STEVE DAWSON

Now let's look at the same procedure applied to a regular hexagon. You may recognize the Escher tessellation in figure 7-35 as the
one featured in his famous lithograph *Reptiles* that we saw earlier
(figure 7-2, page 184).

Fig. 7-35. *Study of Regular Division of the Plane with Reptiles,* M. C. Escher

This design is based on a grid of regular hexagons; residual
traces of Escher's own grid will help us locate all six vertices of a
typical hexagon. We will look at an individual lizard in a single
hexagon to discover how it can be formed (figure 7-36).

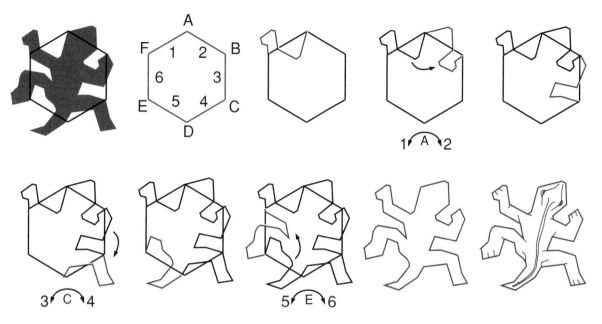

Fig. 7-36. Modifying a hexagon by rotation about vertices to create the lizard shape

We number the sides and letter the vertices of a single hexagon, then study the contour of the lizard within. We find that we can create the lizard shape as follows: modify side 1; rotate this modification about vertex A to side 2; modify side 3; rotate it about vertex C to side 4; modify side 5; rotate it about vertex E to side 6.

The lizard shape thus formed will tessellate in a pattern with three different centers of three-fold rotation, as shown in figure 7-37. That is, a rotation of 120° about each of these three points brings the design into coincidence. (You might trace a lizard and rotate your tracing to verify this relationship.) Can you spot these symmetries in the original tessellation (figure 7-35)?

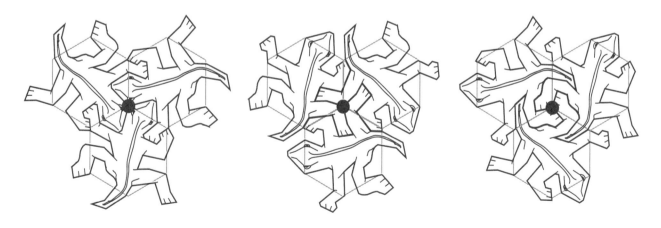

Fig. 7-37. Three centers of three-fold rotational symmetry

Figure 7-38 shows our attempt to create a tessellating shape through this same procedure—modifying a regular hexagon by rotation about vertices. The resulting outline resembles a peg-legged pirate, even before we add interior details. The tessellation of this shape has three centers of three-fold rotation. Can you find them?

Fig. 7-38. A hexagon modified by rotation about vertices

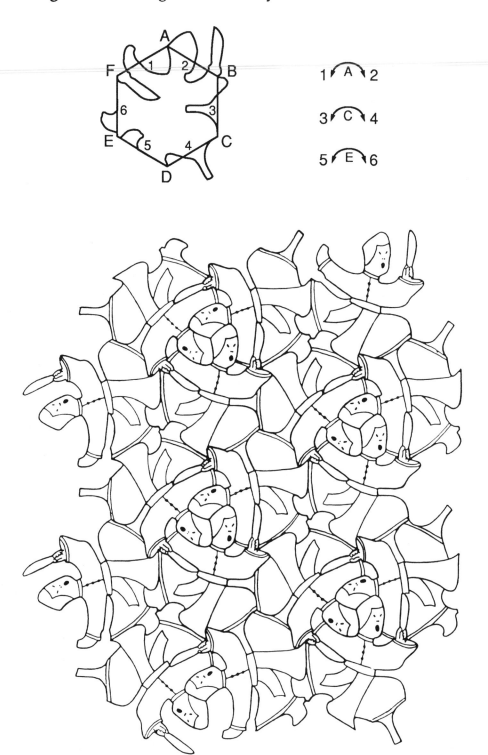

The shape in figure 7-39 was also created from a hexagon with modifications of sides 1, 3, and 5 rotated about vertices to adjacent sides. In this case, the artist made random modifications, then gave three different interpretations to the shapes—a broad-beaked parrot, a crested bird, and a flying squirrel. In the resulting tessellation, identically oriented shapes were given the same interpretation.

Fig. 7-39. A hexagon modified by rotation about vertices

ART BY STEVE DAWSON

The shapes in the next Escher tessellation, figure 7-40, can be created by combining both rotation techniques—rotation about a vertex of a polygon, and rotation about the midpoint of a side of that polygon.

Fig. 7-40. *Birds*, M. C. Escher

Let's look for rotation points in figure 7-40 as we try to discover the underlying polygonal grid. Perhaps most obvious is the center of three-fold rotation where the birds' beaks meet. There are two such points—one for the dark birds and one for the light. The lower tip of each bird's left wing marks another point of rotational symmetry; ignoring the color differences, we see here a center of six-fold rotation. These two kinds of rotation points, six-fold and three-fold, mark the vertices of a grid of equilateral triangles.

Another center of rotational symmetry, overlooked by most observers, is located on the right wing, midway between the beaks of adjacent light and dark birds. This is a center of two-fold rotation; a rotation of 180° brings adjacent birds into coincidence.

Fig. 7-41. A grid of equilateral triangles underlying the *Birds* design

Figure 7-41 shows the underlying grid of equilateral triangles. Note that the points of two-fold rotation lie at the midpoint of one of the sides of each triangle.

Looking at a single triangle from the grid with its inscribed bird, we find that we can modify side 1 and rotate this modification about vertex A to side 2. Since a triangle has an odd number of sides, side 3 has no partner, so we cannot continue to use rotation about a vertex. Instead, we modify *half* of side 3 and rotate the modification 180° about the midpoint of that side. The bird shape is now complete.

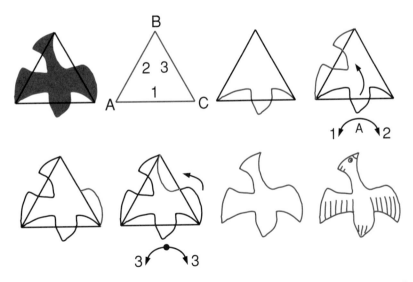

Fig. 7-42. Modifying by rotation about a vertex and rotation about the midpoint of a side to create the bird shape

Now let's see how we might create our own tessellating shape, using the same combination of procedures evident in Escher's *Birds* tessellation. Starting with a triangle, we modify side 1 and rotate that modification around vertex A to side 2. We then modify half of side 3 and rotate that modification 180° about the midpoint of the side. Can you see these changes in figure 7-43? The tessellation of this shape has centers of six-fold, three-fold, and two-fold rotation, as did the Escher *Birds* tessellation. Can you find them all?

Fig. 7-43. An equilateral triangle modified by rotation about a vertex and rotation about the midpoint of a side

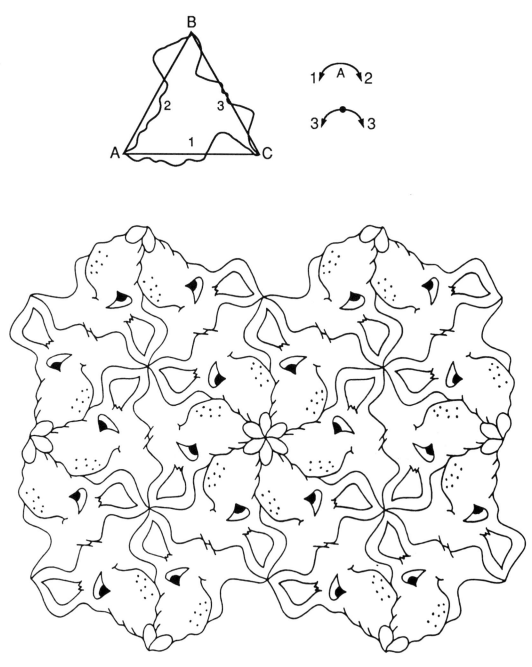

The same combination of procedures was used to create the tessellating shape shown in figure 7-44. The artist made random modifications, then experimented with the six different interpretations shown. The dragon option is shown tessellating Can you find the centers of rotational symmetry?

Fig. 7-44. Another equilateral triangle modified by rotation about a vertex and rotation about the midpoint of a side

duck

bird

mutant horse

goblin

dragon

cuckoo

ART BY STEVE DAWSON

Fig. 7-45. *Lizard IV*, M. C. Escher

The Escher tessellation of lizards in figure 7-45 is similar in design, again combining rotation about a vertex and rotation about the midpoint of a side. Residual traces of the artist's grid, just visible in the figure, reveal that the design is based on an isosceles right triangle rather than an equilateral triangle.

To arrive at this lizard shape, we can follow the steps shown in figure 7-46: we first modify one leg of the triangle, side 1, and rotate this modification about vertex A to the other leg, side 2. Then we modify half of the hypotenuse and rotate this change about the midpoint.

This tessellation has a point of four-fold rotation at the vertex of the right angle, a point of two-fold rotation at the midpoint of the hypotenuse, and as a natural consequence, two points of four-fold rotation at the base vertices, where the heads of either four light or four dark lizards meet.

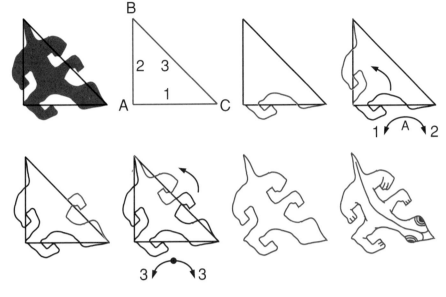

Fig. 7-46. Modifying an isosceles right triangle by rotation about a vertex and rotation about the midpoint of a side to create the lizard shape

We can use the same combination of procedures to modify an isosceles triangle with an angle of 120°. In the resulting tessellation, the rotational symmetry is three-fold—as opposed to six-fold when we start with an equilateral triangle and four-fold when we use an isosceles right triangle. A portion of the grid underlying such a tessellation is shown in figure 7-47, with sides and vertices of each triangle labeled. Here you can clearly see where three angle A's meet at a point of three-fold symmetry and angles B and C come together alternately at a point of six-fold symmetry.

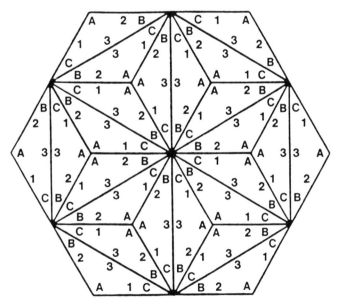

Fig. 7-47. Grid underlying a 120° isosceles triangle tessellation

In figure 7-48, we use these procedures to modify such a triangle, creating a hummingbird that tessellates as shown.

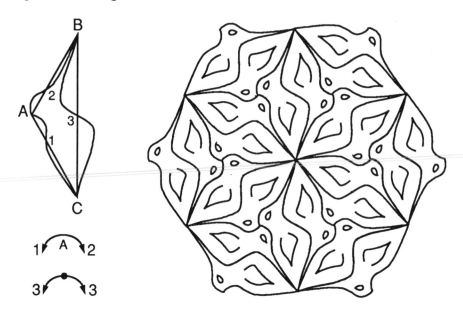

Fig. 7-48. Modifying an isosceles triangle with an angle of 120°

Modifying Polygons by Reflection

Now we take up a new technique involving the transformation that we call reflection. The design we will first study is a tessellation of human figures that appears at the right side of Escher's *Metamorphosis [I]* woodcut (figure 7-49). An enlarged version of this pattern (created with pencil and watercolor prior to use in the woodcut) is shown in figure 7-50.

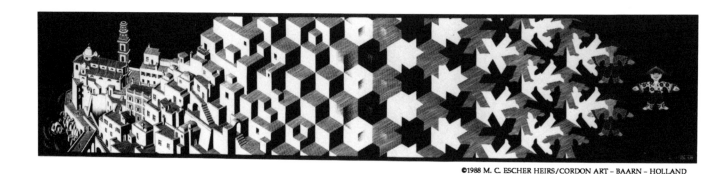

Fig. 7-49. *Metamorphosis [I]* , M. C. Escher

Fig. 7-50. *Study of Regular Division of the Plane with Human Figures*, M. C. Escher

As we see in figure 7-51, this tessellation is based on a grid of isosceles triangles with angles of 120°. However, unlike previous tessellations we have explored, in this case the tessellating shape is created from *two* such triangles. That is, each triangle contains just half of a human figure.

The resulting tessellation has reflective symmetry. Mirror lines (lines of reflection) run in three different directions, tracing out a grid of equilateral triangles. The shortest possible translations are in directions parallel to these mirror lines. The tessellation also has three-fold rotational symmetry. Adjacent human figures can exchange places by a rotation of 120° about the tip of their hats or about the lower end of either sleeve.

Fig. 7-51. A grid of 120° isosceles triangles underlying the human figure design

Figure 7-52 demonstrates how we modify and reflect a triangle to create the desired shape. First we modify side 1 and rotate this modification about vertex A to side 2. Side 3 falls on a mirror line (line of reflection); we simply reflect the modified shape about this line to obtain the other half of the human figure.

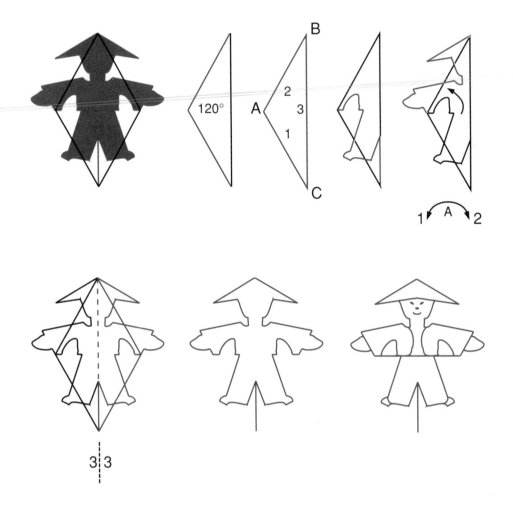

Fig. 7-52. Modifying by rotation about a vertex and reflection to create a human figure

The underlying grid, with the sides and vertices of each triangle labeled according to the orientation of its inscribed human half, is shown again in figure 7-53. Compare this grid with the one in figure 7-47. Both show tessellations with the same triangle—but in each case the triangle is modified by different transformations. Here the triangle has been reflected about side 3; before, side 3 was rotated about its midpoint. You can see the difference by comparing the placement of angles B and C in the two grids.

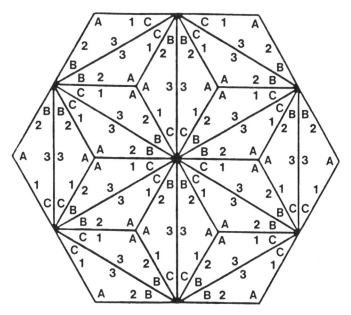

Fig. 7-53. An alternative configuration of 120° isosceles triangles

In figure 7-54, we follow the same pattern of transformations, starting with an isosceles triangle with an angle of 120°: modify side 1 and rotate about vertex A to side 2, then reflect about side 3. The resulting clown face tessellates in a pattern that has both reflective and rotational symmetry.

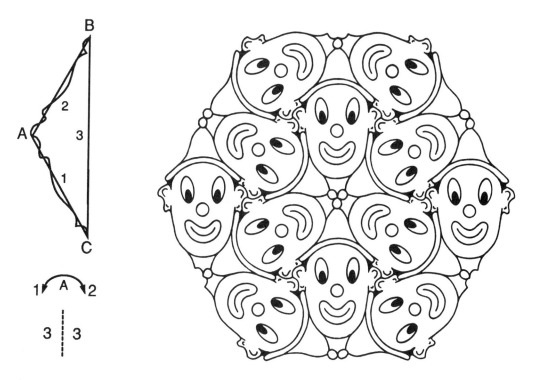

Fig. 7-54. Triangle modified by rotation about a vertex and reflection

Fig. 7-55. *Crabs*, M. C. Escher

For the Escher tessellation of crabs in figure 7-55, the tessellating element was also created by a combination of transformations that includes reflection.

Note that the tessellation is based on a grid of rectangles (figure 7-56). One half of each crab fits in a single rectangle in exactly the same way as all the other corresponding crab halves. Figure 7-57 demonstrates how we can create the crab shape: modify side 2 and translate this modification to side 4; modify half of side 1 and rotate about the midpoint; reflect about side 3, which falls on a mirror line.

The crab tessellation naturally has reflective symmetry. The mirror lines, running vertically from top to bottom, coincide with the mirror lines of the crabs. If we ignore color differences, the shortest possible translations are between adjacent crabs in a direction parallel to the mirror lines.

As we discovered in chapter 4, any tessellation with both translational and reflective symmetry will also have glide-reflection symmetry. You can see that, ignoring color, the tessellation can be made to coincide with itself by reflecting it about any mirror line and then translating it vertically.

If we ignore both color and reflections, we can find points of two-fold rotation in any rectangle, at the vertices that do *not* lie on a mirror line, and at the midpoints of the vertical sides joining those vertices.

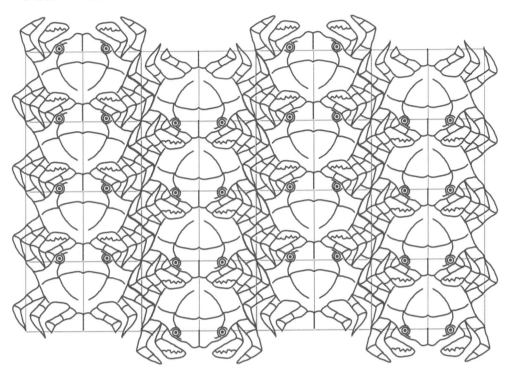

Fig. 7-56. A rectangular grid underlying the *Crabs* design

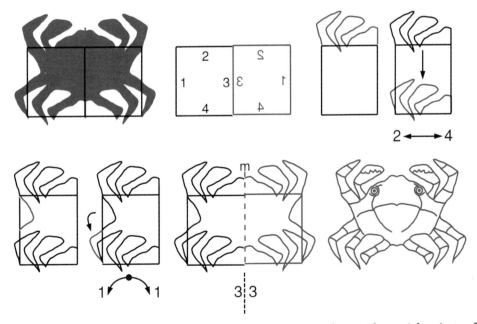

Fig. 7-57. Modifying by translation, rotation about the midpoint of a side, and reflection to create the crab shape

Now let's see how we might create a similar shape ourselves. In figure 7-58, we begin with a rectangle and modify it using the same procedure. The result suggests a devilish visage. The tessellation of this figure has translational symmetry, reflective symmetry, glide-reflection symmetry, and two-fold rotational symmetry.

Fig. 7-58. A rectangle modified by translation, rotation about the midpoint of a side, and reflection

ART BY STEVE DAWSON

The tessellation of dogs shown in figure 7-59 is one of Escher's most ingenious designs. Note how the black dogs' rear toes become teeth for the white dogs, and vice versa.

Fig. 7-59. *Dogs*, M. C. Escher

Let's look for symmetries in this tessellation. It's easy to see that it has translational symmetry. We can bring the tessellation into coincidence with itself by translating horizontally between adjacent dogs (ignoring color) or vertically between dogs of the same color.

If we were to draw vertical lines through the elbows of the white dogs, we would find that these lines also pass through the elbows of the black dogs. A white dog will exchange places with the black dog just below it if we first reflect it about the line just described, then translate it vertically. Thus the tessellation has glide-reflection symmetry. It does *not*, however, have reflective symmetry.

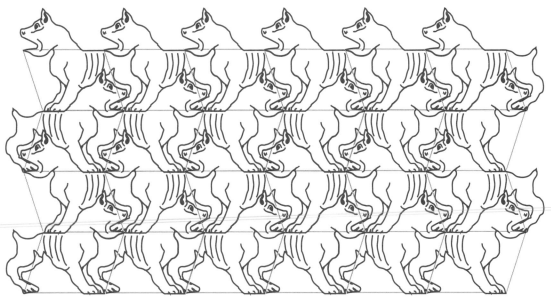

Fig. 7-60. A grid of parallelograms underlying the *Dogs* design

The dog design is based on a grid of parallelograms occurring in two different orientations, as shown in figure 7-60. Figure 7-61 shows the steps we take to create the dog shape. The first step is a simple modification of side 1 translated to side 3. Observe closely what happens next: We modify side 2, then reflect that modification about a vertical line that passes through the center of the parallelogram, and finally translate the reflected modification to side 4. This is the transformation that we call a glide reflection.

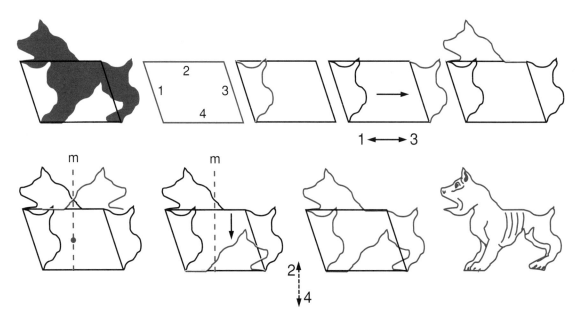

Fig. 7-61. Modifying by translation and glide reflection to create the dog shape

Figure 7-62 illustrates our modification of a parallelogram using the same procedure that produced the dogs for the Escher design. We started with the idea of creating a fish and modified the parallelogram until its contour resembled a fish shape. The tessellation of our fish shape has translational symmetry and glide-reflection symmetry, like the Escher tessellation that inspired it.

Fig. 7-62. A parallelogram modified by translation and glide reflection

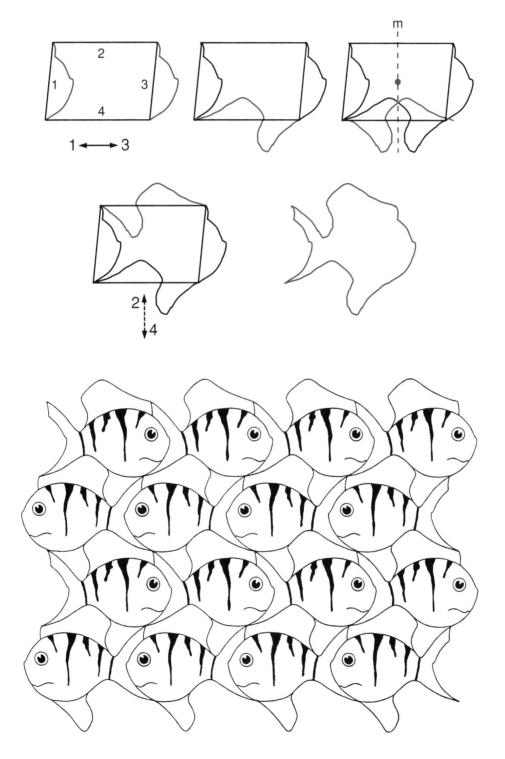

Although we have focused our discussion on designs formed by a single tessellating shape, let's take a look now at the tessellation in figure 7-63, which Escher prepared for use in his lithograph *Encounter*.

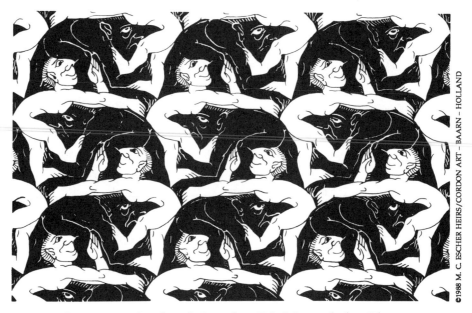

Fig. 7-63. *Study of Regular Division of the Plane with Human Figures*, M. C. Escher

The pattern here is built up from two figures, an optimist (light) and a pessimist (dark), each occurring in two different orientations. If, however, we regard the tessellating shape as a unit containing two figures, an optimist and the pessimist directly below, we find that the tessellation has precisely the same properties as Escher's tessellation of dogs. The two-part tessellating shape is once again a parallelogram modified by translation and glide reflection, as shown in figure 7-64.

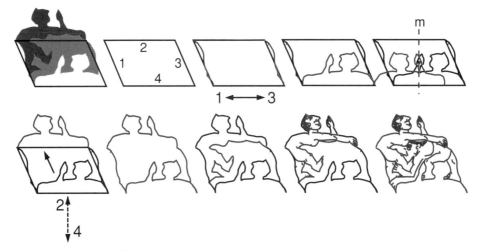

Fig. 7-64. Modifying by translation and glide reflection to create the optimist/pessimist shape

In general, we may always subdivide any tessellating shape into as many figures as suits our fancy.

Now let's consider another design created by glide reflection. The Escher tessellation shown in figure 7-65, which he used in his wood engraving *Swans*, is deceptively simple looking. With its alternating rows of dark and light swans, the pattern has clear translational symmetry; both vertical and horizontal translations bring swans of the same color into coincidence.

The swan tessellation has glide-reflection symmetry without reflective symmetry. A dark swan exchanges places with the light swan just below and to the right of it if we first reflect it about a vertical line midway between the tips of their heads, then translate it vertically. The same is true of a dark swan and the light swan just below and to the left of it.

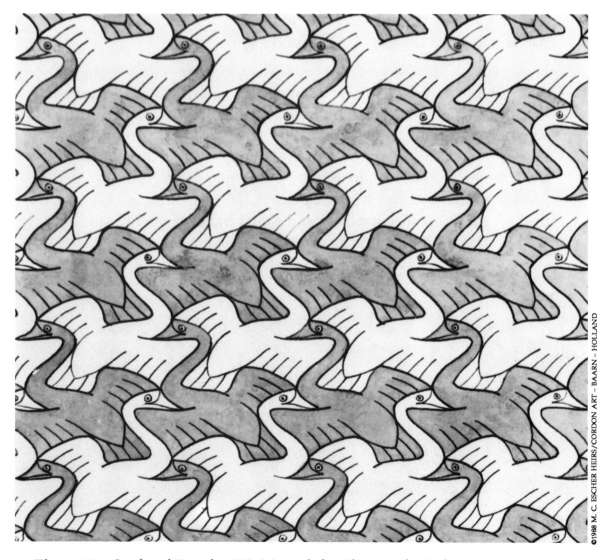

Fig. 7-65. *Study of Regular Division of the Plane with Birds,* M. C. Escher

Fig. 7-66. A kite-shaped quadrilateral grid underlying the *Swans* design

The tessellation is based on a grid of kite-shaped quadrilaterals, as shown in figure 7-66. The vertices of this grid are marked by the tips of the heads of all swans, dark and light. The horizontal diagonal of each quadrilateral subdivides it into two congruent triangular halves, as shown in figure 7-67 (second step).

It takes a bit of work to arrive at the swan shape, but you can follow the step-by-step process in figure 7-67. Starting with our kite-shaped quadrilateral, we modify side 1 and reflect this modification about a vertical line. As you can see in the figure, this mirror line passes through the midpoints of sides 1 and 2. After reflection, we translate the modification to side 2. Then we go through the same process with sides 3 and 4: modify side 3, reflect about a vertical line through the midpoints of sides 3 and 4, and translate the reflected modification to side 4. This gives us the desired swan shape.

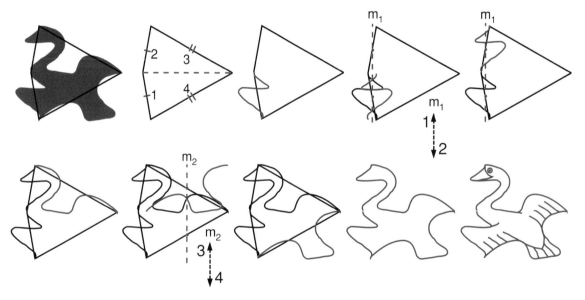

Fig. 7-67. Modifying by glide reflection to create the swan shape

Following the same pattern of transformations, we can create our own tessellating shape from a kite-shaped quadrilateral, as shown in figure 7-68. We started with the intent of creating a dog and modified the sides of the quadrilateral through glide reflection until it looked something like a dog. Like the Escher swan design, the tessellation of this dog has translational symmetry and glide-reflection symmetry, but no reflective symmetry.

Fig. 7-68. Modifying a quadrilateral by glide reflection

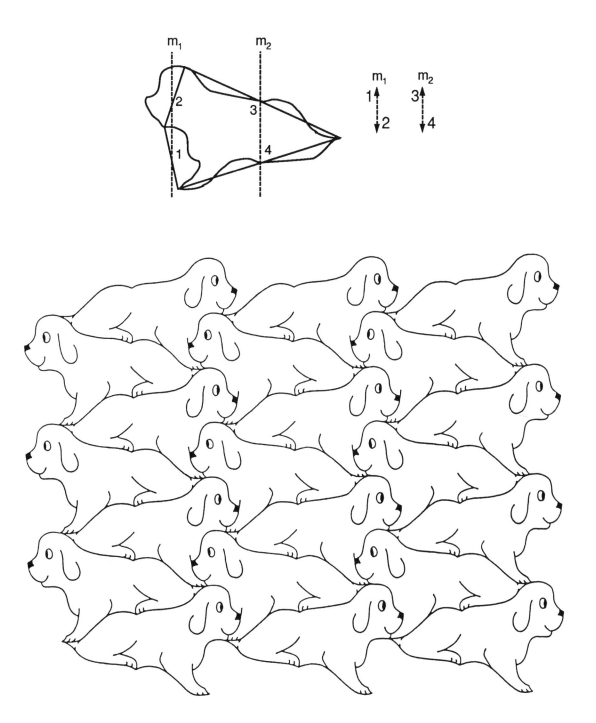

The same approach was used to create the tessellating owls and seals in figure 7-69, modifying two kite-shaped quadrilaterals (one convex, one concave) by glide reflection. The artist in these cases worked with no particular shape in mind, adding details to interpret the figures after the fact.

Fig. 7-69. Two more examples of modifying quadrilaterals by glide reflection

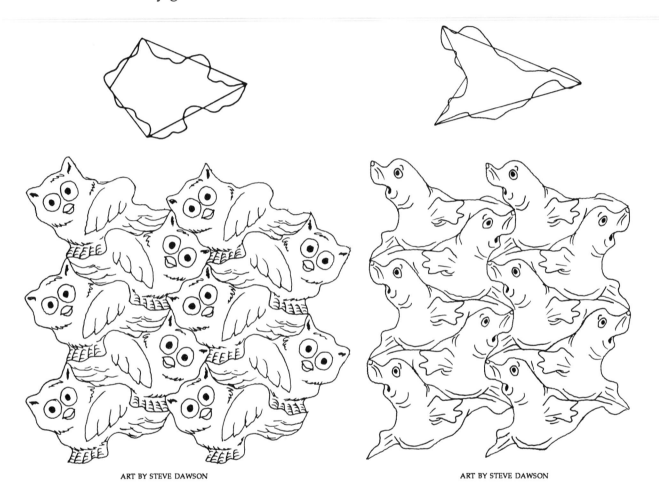

ART BY STEVE DAWSON   ART BY STEVE DAWSON

The same approach can also be used to create the tessellating shape in figure 7-70, which Escher devised for use in his woodcut *Horseman*. The creation of the horseman's contour is perhaps the best illustration of Escher's cunning ingenuity. Figure 7-71 details how we can arrive at this shape. After modifying side 1 of an appropriate kite-shaped quadrilateral, we reflect it about the vertical line passing through the midpoints of sides 1 and 2, then translate the reflected modification up to side 2. Then we modify side 3, reflect it about the

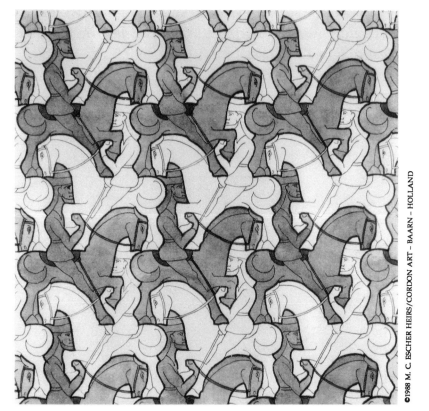

Fig. 7-70. *Study of Regular Division of the Plane with Horsemen*, M. C. Escher

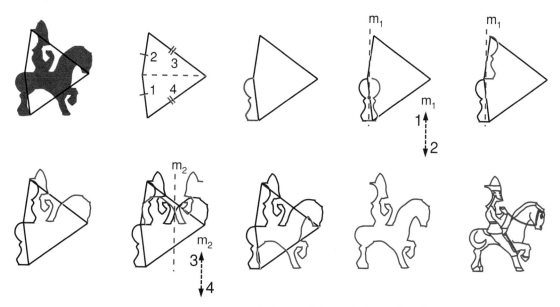

Fig. 7-71. Modifying a quadrilateral by glide reflection to create the horseman shape

through the midpoints of sides 3 and 4, and translate this reflected modification to side 4. This completes the horseman shape.

Each of the convex kite-shaped quadrilaterals we have just seen modified could be subdivided into two isosceles triangles by drawing the vertical diagonal, as shown in figure 7-72.

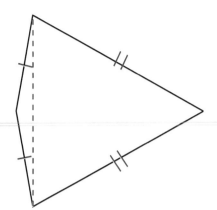

Fig. 7-72. A convex kite-shaped quadrilateral subdivided into two isosceles triangles

When we modified such a quadrilateral to create, for example, Escher's horseman, the isosceles triangle on the left was modified by glide reflection, as was the isosceles triangle on the right. This would suggest that we might be able to use the glide-reflection procedure with a tessellating grid of isosceles triangles.

But a triangle has three sides. If we modify the legs of an isosceles triangle by glide reflection, how do we deal with the third side? We have two choices available: reflecting the modified triangle about the third side, or rotating it about the midpoint of the third side. With the hummingbird design (figure 7-48) we rotated it; with the clown face (figure 7-54) we reflected it.

In figure 7-73, the selected isosceles triangle is equilateral. We have modified sides 1 and 2 by glide reflection, using a sequence of steps identical to that we just used to create Escher's horseman. Then, we modified half of side 3 and rotated this change 180° about the midpoint of the side. The resulting contour resembles a bird even without the addition of interior details. Our bird tessellates in a design that has translational symmetry, glide-reflection symmetry, and two-fold rotational symmetry.

Figure 7-74 shows another isosceles triangle, in this case *not* equilateral, modified by the same transformations. Rotated counter-clockwise 90°, the modified triangle could be interpreted as a glamorous lady pig.

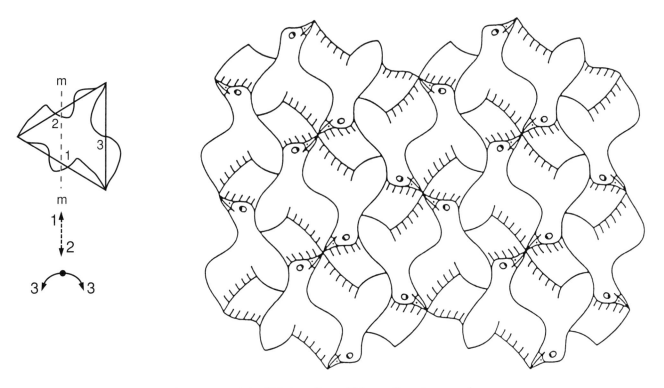

Fig. 7-73. Modifying by glide reflection and rotation about the midpoint of a side

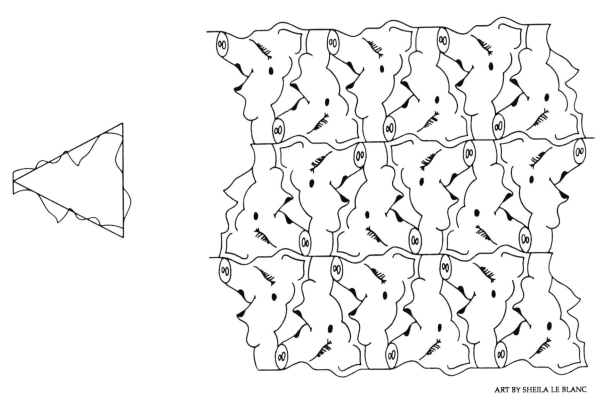

Fig. 7-74. Another triangle modified by glide reflection and rotation about the midpoint of a side

In this chapter we have merged two approaches to exploring tessellations of animate figures; both can lead you into some fascinating explorations of your own. One approach is to analyze an existing design—perhaps one of the many by Escher that we have not presented here. What was the generating polygon? How was it modified? What are the symmetries of the tessellation? Such an analysis can be accomplished by locating the underlying grid of polygons. The vertices of those polygons are usually points of rotational symmetry. Other visual clues may reveal translations or glide reflections.

A second approach is to create your own designs, starting with a tessellating polygonal shape, then modifying sides or half-sides and transforming these modifications to other parts of the polygon. You might have some specific object in mind and modify the polygon until its contour resembles that object, or you might modify the polygon with random curves and interpret the resulting shape by adding interior details. Working towards a decent contour requires tenacity, but the effort will make you better appreciate the challenge. As Escher's son George has advised us:

> Do not confuse the creation of a meaningful contour with the highlighting of the interior of a tile. These are fundamentally different things. Almost anyone can take a random shape and draw something life-like inside its outline.

  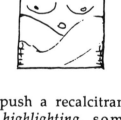

> But it is an entirely different story to push a recalcitrant outline into a pattern that suggests, *without highlighting,* some living thing. Highlighting may be necessary to clarify a decision: is it a bird or a fish? But it is often not even necessary, if the contour is characteristic enough.

> This discussion is not new. It is a repeat of a homily given to me by my father when I was around twelve years old and had made some tessellations like the above. "Look, it is not that difficult," I told him. "Why do you work so hard on such a simple task?" I soon found out.

> — George Escher
> (letter to J. Britton, Sept. 1987)

Designing an Escher-like shape and drawing its tessellation is a time-consuming yet satisfying exercise. Following are some practical tips to help you get started.

A scalene quadrilateral allows you the greatest freedom and flexibility when you attempt your first design. As you make your preliminary sketches, you may find that you want to alter the shape of your original polygon—and with a scalene quadrilateral, you can. However long its sides and whatever the size of its angles, a quadrilateral will tessellate the plane if each of the sides is rotated 180° about its midpoint. (The only drawback of a scalene quadrilateral is the relative difficulty of drawing its tessellating grid, but if you tessellate by the first method we suggest below, this is not a problem.)

Once your preliminary sketch is completed, you must prepare an accurate version of the shape for your tessellation. One simple and practical approach is to cut the original polygon shape from construction paper or lightweight cardboard, then cut appropriate "holes" and tape them on as corresponding "bumps" to represent your modifications. (In the case of glide reflection, you will need to flip the bump before taping.) You can mark the location of simple details with slits or small holes in your final shape.

To create the tessellation, position your pattern on another sheet of paper, trace about its perimeter, and mark the location of interior details. By repositioning and tracing the pattern again and again, you will see the tessellation evolve before your eyes.

A more precise procedure involves no cutting and allows you more freedom in adding interior details—but it also requires more time and patience, and either a light table or a window that you can draw against. You will need three sheets of translucent paper. Draw your polygon on two of these. Then, on one polygon, draw your modifications to the sides in *one* of their two locations. Tape this polygon to a window or light table and superimpose the second polygon precisely on top. Trace your initial modifications, then move the superimposed sheet as needed to locate and trace each modification in its new location. (For glide reflection, you will need to flip the base polygon.) You end up with an accurately drawn shape to serve as your pattern, to which you can add interior details at will.

Now you need to create the underlying grid for your tessellating polygon. To avoid the problem of grid lines in your finished design, we suggest drawing the *mirror image* of the grid on the *back* of the third sheet of translucent paper. That way, when you tape this sheet face up over your pattern at the window or a light table, you can see the grid lines to help you position your shape, but they will not appear in your final drawing. (Alternatively, of course, you could draw the grid on a separate sheet and draw your final design on yet another sheet placed over it—but three sheets of paper start to get opaque, even with a light table.)

From here on, completing the drawing is simply a matter of meticulous tracing. You align a polygon in the grid precisely with the polygon of your pattern, then trace all marks *except the polygon* on the top sheet. Select an adjacent polygon, turn the sheet to align with the pattern, and trace—continuing in this manner until you are satisfied with the extent of your tessellation.

For either method—tracing around a cardboard pattern or through translucent paper—ink gives you better contrast than pencil, but slips and errors are harder to repair. If you use pencil, you can improve the contrast as follows: Photocopy your final drawing, process it at a slow setting through a thermal transparency maker, then photocopy the resultant acetate. The improvement in quality can be quite dramatic.

Whether you undertake the creation of an Escher-like drawing or turn to Escher's own art to further analyze his tessellations, the fundamental procedures that we have presented in this chapter give you all the necessary tools for these exciting investigations. We hope we have inspired you to explore further.

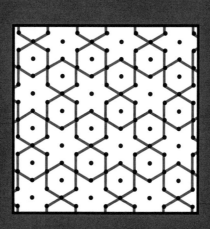

DOT PAPER
&
SKETCHING
GRIDS

INTRODUCTION TO TESSELLATIONS • Copyright © by Dale Seymour Publications

INTRODUCTION TO TESSELLATIONS • Copyright © by Dale Seymour Publications

INTRODUCTION TO TESSELLATIONS • Copyright © by Dale Seymour Publications

Appendix

Algebraic Analysis of Regular Polygons Around a Point

In chapter 3 we noted that there are 17 possible *combinations* of regular polygons around a vertex, and with these there are a total of 21 different *arrangements*. This section gives an algebraic analysis of these results.

Since the smallest possible angle in any regular polygon is 60° (in a triangle), we cannot have more than six polygons meeting at any vertex. Also, we cannot have fewer than three polygons at any vertex. Therefore we are interested in investigating the cases where 3, 4, 5, and 6 angles meet at a point. Recall that the measure of any angle of a regular polygon with n sides and n angles is generalized by the expression

$$\frac{(n - 2)\,180°}{n}$$

The sum of the angles around any vertex is 360°. Thus, if we consider three polygons with n_1, n_2, and n_3 sides, we have

$$\left(\frac{n_1 - 2}{n_1} + \frac{n_2 - 2}{n_2} + \frac{n_3 - 2}{n_3}\right)180° = 360°$$

This expression can be simplified to

$$\frac{1}{n_1} + \frac{1}{n_2} + \frac{1}{n_3} = \frac{1}{2}$$

Similarly, we find the arrangements for four polygons gives the equation

$$\frac{1}{n_1} + \frac{1}{n_2} + \frac{1}{n_3} + \frac{1}{n_4} = 1$$

Arrangements for five polygons gives

$$\frac{1}{n_1} + \frac{1}{n_2} + \frac{1}{n_3} + \frac{1}{n_4} + \frac{1}{n_5} = \frac{3}{2}$$

And finally, for six polygons we have the equation

$$\frac{1}{n_1} + \frac{1}{n_2} + \frac{1}{n_3} + \frac{1}{n_4} + \frac{1}{n_5} + \frac{1}{n_6} = 2$$

These four equations have 17 possible solutions, as shown in figure A-1. Although we found 21 arrangements (illustrated in chapter 3, page 52), recall that the four additional arrangements are simply repeated polygon combinations in a different order. (These are marked with * in the chart.)

No.	n_1	n_2	n_3	No.	n_1	n_2	n_3	n_4	n_5	n_6
1	3	7	42	10	6	6	6			
2	3	8	24	11*	3	3	4	12		
3	3	9	18	12*	3	3	6	6		
4	3	10	15	13*	3	4	4	6		
5	3	12	12	14	4	4	4	4		
6	4	5	20	15*	3	3	3	4	4	
7	4	6	12	16	3	3	3	3	6	
8	4	8	8	17	3	3	3	3	3	3
9	5	5	10							

Fig. A-1. The 17 possible regular polygon combinations

Of the 17 arrangements, three are the regular tessellations (triangles, squares, and hexagons.) Six of the remaining 14 cannot be extended to tessellate the entire plane. That leaves us with the eight semiregular tessellations. The 3.3.4.12 is actually the 4.6.12 with two threes (60°) in place of a six (120°). One of the eight semiregular tessellations differs from the other seven in that it exists in two mirror-symmetric forms, as shown in figure A-2.

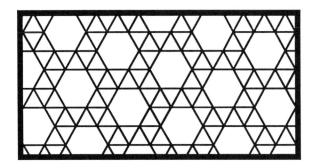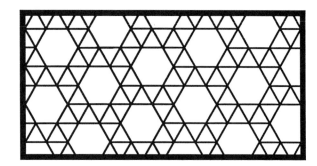

Fig. A-2. Two different forms of semiregular tessellation 3.3.3.3.6

Glossary

Acute angle   An angle that measures less than 90°.

Acute triangle   A triangle with three acute angles.

Adjacent angles   Angles that share a common side and a common vertex point.

Angle of rotation   The measure (size) of the angle of a figure's rotation about a point in a plane.

Center of rotation   A point about which a figure is rotated.

Centroid of a polygon   The center of gravity or balancing point of a figure.

Closed figure   A figure in a plane whose boundary starts at a point and comes back to that same point.

Concave polygon   A polygon containing one or more interior angles that measure greater than 180° (but less than 360°).

Congruent angles   Angles that have the same measure.

Congruent polygons   Polygons that have the same size and shape.

Convex polygon   A polygon containing *no* interior angles that measure greater than 180°.

Decagon   A polygon with ten sides.

Diamond   A parallelogram formed by joining two equilateral triangles of the same size along an edge.

Dihex   A shape formed by combining two regular hexagons of the same size along an edge.

Dodecagon   A polygon with twelve sides.

Dual tessellation   Two tessellations, each formed by connecting the centroids of the other.

Endpoints   Points at the ends of a line segment.

Equiangular triangle   A triangle with all three angles congruent (of equal measure).

Equilateral triangle   A triangle with all three sides congruent (of equal length).

Exterior angle (of a polygon)   An angle on the exterior of a polygon formed at a vertex by two adjacent sides, one of which has been extended.

Four-fold rotational symmetry   Characteristic of a figure that coincides with itself after a 90° (360°/4) rotation about a point.

Glide reflection   A transformation that moves a figure in a slide and also mirrors it.

Glide reflection symmetry   Characteristic of a figure that coincides with itself after an appropriate reflection and translation.

Heptagon   A polygon with seven sides.

Hexagon   A polygon with six sides.

Hexiamond A shape formed by combining six equilateral triangles of the same size along their edges.

Inscribed polygon A polygon whose vertices all lie on a given figure.

Interior angle (of a polygon) An angle in the interior of a polygon formed by two adjacent sides.

Isosceles triangle A triangle with two congruent sides.

Kite A quadrilateral with two pairs of congruent sides of different lengths and one pair of equal angles.

Lattice An arrangement of points in a given geometric pattern.

Line of reflection A line in a plane that lies equidistant from any two corresponding opposite points in a figure that has reflective symmetry; also called *mirror line*.

Line segment A connected portion of a straight line.

Magnitude of a translation The distance a point travels in the direction of a given translation.

Median of a triangle A line joining a vertex of a triangle with the midpoint of the opposite side.

Midpoint of a line segment The point equidistant from the ends of the segment.

Mosaic Synonym for tessellation or tiling.

N-fold rotational symmetry Characteristic of a figure that coincides with itself after a $360°/n$ rotation about a point.

N-gon A polygon with n sides.

Nonagon A polygon with nine sides.

Obtuse angle An angle that measures more than 90° but less than 180°.

Obtuse triangle A triangle with one obtuse angle.

Octagon A polygon with eight sides.

Parallel lines Two or more lines in the same plane that do not intersect, even if extended.

Parallelogram A quadrilateral whose opposite sides are congruent and parallel.

Pentagon A polygon with five sides.

Pentahexes Shapes formed by joining five regular hexagons of the same size along their edges.

Pentiamond A shape formed by combining five equilateral triangles of the same size along their edges.

Pentominoes Shapes formed by joining five squares of the same size along their edges.

Perigon The angle of one complete rotation (360°).

Perpendicular lines Lines that meet at right angles in a plane.

Plane (surface) A two-dimensional, flat surface that is infinite.

Polygon A simple closed shape, bounded by line segments.

Polyhexes A classification of shapes formed by combining two or more regular hexagons of the same size along their edges.

Polyiamonds   A classification of shapes formed by combining two or more equilateral triangles of the same size along their edges.

Polyominoes   A classification of shapes created by combining two or more congruent squares of the same size along their edges.

Quadrilateral   A polygon with four sides.

Rectangle   A quadrilateral that contains four right angles.

Reflection (in a plane)   A transformation that mirrors a figure in a plane.

Reflex angle   An angle that measures more than 180° but less than 360°.

Regular polygon   A polygon with all its sides congruent and all its angles congruent.

Regular tessellation   A plane tessellation of one type of regular polygon, each such polygon being the same size.

Rhombus   An equilateral quadrilateral.

Right angle   An angle that measures 90°.

Right triangle   A triangle that contains one right angle.

Rotation (in a plane)   A transformation that turns a figure about a point in a plane.

Scalene triangle   A triangle with sides of three different lengths.

Semiregular tessellation   A tessellation of two or more regular polygons, with edges of equal length, that has an identical combination of polygons at every vertex point.

Six-fold rotational symmetry   Characteristic of a figure that coincides with itself after a 60° (360°/6) rotation about a point.

Star polygon   A star-shaped polygon containing two sets of congruent interior angles.

Straight angle   An angle that measures 180°.

Symmetry   Characteristic of a figure that can be made to coincide with itself by a translation, rotation, reflection, or glide reflection.

Tangent circles   Circles that intersect at one point only.

Tessellation (plane)   A covering of an infinite plane, without any gaps or overlaps, by a pattern of one or more congruent shapes.

Tessellation (space)   A filling of space, without any gaps or overlaps, by a pattern of one or more three-dimensional shapes.

Tetrahexes   Shapes formed by combining four regular hexagons of the same size along their edges.

Tetriamond   A shape formed by combining four equilateral triangles of the same size along their edges.

Three-fold rotational symmetry   Characteristic of a figure that coincides with itself after a 120° (360°/3) rotation about a point.

Tiling   Synonym for tessellation or mosaic.

Transformation   In this book, a movement of a figure to a new location, leaving the figure unchanged in size and shape.

Translation   A transformation involving a slide of a rigid figure without rotation.

Translational symmetry   Characteristic of a figure that coincides with itself after an appropriate translation (slide).

Trapezoid   A quadrilateral with exactly two parallel sides.

Triamond   A shape formed by joining three equilateral triangles of the same size along their edges.

Trihexes   Shapes formed by combining three regular hexagons of the same size along their edges.

Two-fold rotational symmetry   Characteristic of a figure that coincides with itself after a 180° (360°/2) rotation about a point.

Undecagon   A polygon with eleven sides.

Uniform tilings   The three regular and eight semiregular tessellations.

Vertex (of a polygon)   The point of intersection of any two adjacent sides of the polygon.

Vertex (of an angle)   The point of intersection of the two rays that form the angle.

Vertex point (of a tessellation)   Any point in the tessellation where tessellation shapes share a common vertex.

Vertices   Plural of *vertex*.

Bibliography

General Tessellation Designs

Bezuszka, S., M. Kenney, and L. Silvey. 1978. *Designs from Mathematical Patterns*. Palo Alto, CA: Creative Publications.
Explores the application of mathematics to design with activities that relate number patterns to tessellations. Reproducible. Grade 6 to adult. 208 pp.

————. 1977. *Tessellations: The Geometry of Patterns*. Palo Alto, CA: Creative Publications.
Elementary lessons and practice exercises involving basic tessellations. Reproducible. Grade 5 to adult. 170 pp.

Kenney, M., and S. Bezuszka. 1987. *Tessellations Using Logo*. Palo Alto, CA: Dale Seymour Publications.
Collection of 71 activities using Terrapin Logo as a tool for sketching simple and complex tessellations, including Escher-like tessellations. Grade 7 to adult. Reproducible. 96 pp.

Oliver, J. 1979. *Polysymetrics*. Norfolk, England: Tarquin Publications.
Tips on creating simple and complex geometric tilings, with faint-line grids for drawing original patterns. Grade 7 to adult. 40 pp.

Pasternack, M., and L. Silvey. 1974. *Pattern Blocks Coloring Book*. Palo Alto, CA: Creative Publications.
A collection of tessellation patterns, ranging from simple to intricate, that can be created with actual pattern blocks. Grades K-8. 64 pp.

Seymour, D. 1989. *Tessellation Teaching Masters*. Palo Alto, CA: Dale Seymour Publications.
A resource for teacher or student, with full-page designs suitable for transparencies or worksheets. Includes tessellations of regular and nonregular polygons; semiregular tessellations; patterns with star polygons, polyominoes, letters, and nonpolygonal shapes; designs based on duals; and Islamic art. With sketching grids and templates to aid in drawing new designs. Grade 6 to adult. 288 pp.

Symmetry

Stevens, P. S. 1981. *Handbook of Regular Patterns*. Cambridge, MA: MIT Press.
A comprehensive study of symmetry by an architect and artist, delving into the structural anatomy of patterns, how they are generated, and how their parts interrelate. Illustrates designs from textiles, pottery, brick and tile work, mosaics, building plans, and natural forms, as well as Escher prints and drawings. Grade 10 to adult. 404 pp.

Tarasov, L. 1986. *This Amazingly Symmetrical World*. Moscow: Mir Publishers.
An introduction to geometrical symmetry; relates symmetry and asymmetry to the science of our physical world. Grade 11 to adult. 170 pp.

Tessellation Art of Various Cultures

Albarn, K., J. M. Smith, S. Steele, and D. Walker. 1974. *The Language of Pattern*. New York: Harper and Row Publishers, Inc.
A study of decorative pattern by four designers, showing how even the most complex patterns are built from simple basic structures. Includes a section on Islamic constructions. Two-color illustrations. Grade 10 to adult. 112 pp.

Bain, G. 1973. *Celtic Art: The Methods of Construction*. New York: Dover Publications, Inc.
An illustrator's survey of the geometric principles on which the patterns of Celtic art are based. Includes the tessellating Celtic "Key Patterns." Grade 10 to adult. 160 pp.

Bourgoin, J. 1985. *Arabic Allover Patterns*. New York: Dover Publications, Inc.
A resource of 46 full-page tessellating Arabic patterns, coloring-book style, for analysis or inspiration. Grade 6 to adult. 48 pp.

————. 1973. *Arabic Geometrical Pattern and Design*. New York: Dover Publications, Inc.
A collection of 190 designs illustrating the wide range of Islamic geometric art. Contains pages with dotted construction lines for creating original patterns. Grade 7 to adult. 224 pp.

————. 1977. *Islamic Patterns*. New York: Dover Publications, Inc.
A resource of 45 full-page tessellating Islamic patterns, coloring-book style, for analysis or inspiration. Grades 6 and up. 48 pp.

Critchlow, K. 1976. *Islamic Patterns*. New York: Schocken Books.
An analysis of the geometric patterns of Islamic art, exploring the mathematics and construction of these tessellating designs. Two-color illustrations. Grade 10 to adult. 192 pp.

Dye, D. S. 1974. *Chinese Lattice Designs*. New York: Dover Publications, Inc.
Over 1200 illustrations of the geometric and tessellating patterns found in the window lattices on Chinese houses. Grade 9 to adult. 476 pp.

El-Said, I. and A. Parman. 1976. *Geometric Concepts in Islamic Art*. Palo Alto, CA: Dale Seymour Publications.
A pictorial study of Islamic art and the geometry underlying its creation. Grade 10 to adult. 176 pp.

Islamic Art. [Undated.] New York: Metropolitan Museum of Art.
An overview of characteristic Islamic art, with many photos of the intricate geometric patterns found in glass, pottery, weaving, goldwork, paintings, wood paneling, tiles, and sculpture. Grade 9 to adult. 48 pp.

Lukens, M. G. 1965. *Islamic Art.* New York: Metropolitan Museum of Art.
A guide to the museum's Islamic art collection, with historical background. Black-and-white photos throughout. Grade 9 to adult. 48 pp.

Parker, K. 1981. *Contemporary Quilts.* Trumansburg, NY: The Crossing Press.
A selection of original quilt patterns based on the tessellations of M. C. Escher. Grade 6 to adult. 128 pp.

Racinet, A. 1988. *The Encyclopedia of Ornament.* New York: Portland House.
Reproduction of a century-old study of the decorative arts around the world, including Assyrian, ancient Greek, Etruscan, Greco-Roman, Japanese, Persian, Indian, Arabian, Byzantine, and Celtic ornamentation. One hundred full-color plates show a variety of geometric designs. Oversize (approximately 9" x 14"). Grade 9 to adult. 290 pp.

Vasarely, V. 1974. *Vasarely III.* Switzerland: Éditions du Griffon Neuchatel.
Spectacular full-color illustrations of Vasarely's works, including many 3-D geometric patterns. Oversize (approximately 11" x 12"). Grade 7 to adult. 248 pp.

Willson, J. 1983. *Mosaic and Tessellated Patterns.* New York: Dover Publications, Inc.
A set of 32 full-page tessellations, coloring-book style, plus a well-illustrated discussion of different types and how to form them. Grade 7 to adult. 64 pp.

Geometric Transformations and Constructions

Brown, R. G. 1973. *Transformational Geometry.* Palo Alto, CA: Dale Seymour Publications.
An introduction to the algebra and geometry of transformations (including reflections, translations, and rotations), all of which are useful in creating tessellations, particularly Escher-type tessellations. Textbook format (paperback). Grade 9 to adult. 92 pp.

Posamentier, A. S., and W. Wernick. 1988. *Advanced Geometric Constructions.* Palo Alto, CA: Dale Seymour Publications.
A challenging look at constructions using only a straightedge and compass, presenting 19 basic constructions and applying them in unusual problems. Includes separate chapters on triangle and circle constructions. Grade 9 to adult. 102 pp.

Seymour, D. 1988. *Geometric Design*. Palo Alto, CA: Dale Seymour Publications.
A wordless (entirely visual) presentation of the step-by-step construction of more than 80 designs based on triangles, hexagons, squares, octagons, pentagons, and decagons. Includes polygonal templates and masters for sketching original designs. Grade 6 to adult. 136 pp.

Seymour, D., and R. Schadler. 1974. *Creative Constructions*. Palo Alto, CA: Creative Publications.
A collection of more than 250 geometric designs that can be constructed with a straightedge and compass. Includes detailed explanations of constructing the six basic polygons on which the designs are based. Grade 6 to adult. 62 pp.

The Art of M. C. Escher

Bool, F. H., J. R. Kist, J. L. Locher, and F. Wierda. 1981. *M. C. Escher: His Life and Complete Graphic Work*. New York: Harry N. Abrams, Inc.
A detailed biography and complete record of Escher's graphic art. Contains a comprehensive catalog of his works, with descriptions and additional information about some 450 prints that are largely unknown or rarely reproduced. 600 illustrations. Grade 7 to adult. 354 pp.

Coxeter, H. S. M., M. Emmer, R. Penrose, and M. L. Teuber. 1986. *M. C. Escher: Art and Science*. New York: Elsevier Science Publishing Co., Inc.
Articles from the proceedings of an interdisciplinary congress devoted to Escher's work and its relationship to mathematics (including symmetry and geometry), computer graphics, art, science, and the humanities. Grade 10 to adult. 404 pp.

Ernst, B. 1985. *The Magic Mirror of M. C. Escher*. Norfolk: Tarquin Publications.
A detailed description of the conception and execution of Escher's most popular prints, with sketches and diagrams showing how the artist arrived at his astonishing creations. Grade 7 to adult. 116 pp.

Escher, M. C. 1971. *The World of M. C. Escher*. New York: Harry N. Abrams, Inc.
A comprehensive survey of Escher's work. Includes 300 sketches and prints, Escher's essay "Approaches to Infinity," several articles about his work, and a catalog listing of prints. Grade 7 to adult. 268 pp.

————. 1967. *The Graphic Work of M. C. Escher*. New York: Ballantine Books.
Seventy-six of Escher's designs, classified into nine categories to represent specific concepts, such as mirror images (reflections) and divisions of a plane (tessellations). Introduced and explained by the artist. Grade 7 to adult. 96 pp.

Giftwraps by Artists: M. C. Escher. 1987. New York: Harry N. Abrams, Inc.
Sixteen full-color Escher designs on giftwrap paper. Each sheet folds out to approximately 20" x 26". Includes a brief discussion of Escher's art. All ages. 24 pp.

MacGillavry, C. 1976. *Fantasy and Symmetry: The Periodic Drawings of M. C. Escher.* New York: Harry N. Abrams, Inc.
An exploration of the laws underlying different types of tessellations, with 41 of Escher's prints and drawings. 84 pp.

Ranucci, E. R., and J. L. Teeters. 1977. *Creating Escher-Type Drawings.* Palo Alto, CA: Creative Publications.
A how-to book presenting the principles of plane tessellations, symmetry, and the transformations used to create Escher-type designs, with worksheets and grids for practicing the techniques presented. Includes a chapter on analyzing Escher's tessellations. Grade 6 to adult. 200 pp.

Schattschneider, D., and W. Walker. 1987. *M. C. Escher Kaleidocycles.* Corte Madera, CA: Pomegranate Artbooks.
A kit that turns Escher's art into bold, symmetric 3-D paper sculpture with 17 full-color, punch-out models, accompanied by a book that explores the symmetries and mathematical bases of many of Escher's prints. 60 pp.

Advanced Resources

Grünbaum, B., and G. C. Shephard. 1987. *Tilings and Patterns.* New York: W. H. Freeman and Co.
A comprehensive and systematic treatment of tilings and patterns. Focuses on classification and enumeration of tilings and includes detailed surveys of tilings by polygons. Rigorous. Grade 12 to adult. 710 pp.

Pearce, P. 1978. *Structure in Nature Is a Strategy for Design.* Cambridge, MA: MIT Press.
An exploration of the structural designs that occur in nature and their relevance to the design of man-made structures. Explores forms based on triangles, hexagons, and polyhedra. Grade 10 (gifted) to adult. 246 pp.

Sykes, M. 1912. *A Source Book of Problems for Geometry.* Boston: Allyn and Bacon.
A resource originally designed for high school mathematics teachers, exploring how geometric constructions are used to create tiled designs in floors, church steeples, windows, arches, and trusses. With many small, detailed illustrations. Grade 10 to adult. 146 pp.

Illustration Credits

Unless otherwise credited, illustrations were provided by the authors and the staff of Dale Seymour Publications.

CHAPTER 1

Figure 1-9. [Regular Division of the Plane with Birds], M. C. Escher [April 1949]. Wood engraving. Reprinted by permission of Cordon Art.

Figures 1-12 and 1-13. Based on designs in Sykes, (1912), pages 33 and 48.

Figure 1-18. From Barré, Louis. *Herculanum et Pompei*, vol. V, plate 3 (Paris, 1863–70). In Sykes (1912), page 73.

Figure 1-19. From Sykes (1912), page 101.

Figure 1-21. Based on the "Kaleidoscopic Fantasies" wall hanging created by the Kaleidoscopic Quilters Guild of Lemon Grove, California, January 1988. Design recreated from a photo in *Quilting Today*, no. 7, June/July 1988, page 5.

Figure 1-22. From Laura Wheeler Designs "Crocheted Medallions, Pattern 1842."

Figure 1-23. From Sykes (1912), page 16.

Figure 1-24. From Sykes (1912), page 135.

Figure 1-25. From a brochure of The HEXAN Co., Owner Built Homes, page 3.

Figure 1-26. *Sun and Moon*, M. C. Escher. April 1948. Woodcut. Reprinted by permission of Cordon Art.

Figure 1-27. From Larcher, Jean. *Geometrical Designs and Optical Art: 70 Original Drawings* (New York: Dover Publications, 1974), page 37.

CHAPTER 7

Figure 7-1. Copy of mosaics in the Alhambra. M. C. Escher. 1936. Pencil and colored crayon. Reprinted by permission of Cordon Art.

Figure 7-2. *Reptiles*. M. C. Escher. 1943. Lithograph. Reprinted by permission of Cordon Art.

Figure 7-4. [Pegasus] M. C. Escher (Motif used for tiled façade for the Liberal Christian Lyceum in The Hague, executed in concrete in two colors.) Reprinted by permission of Cordon Art.

Figure 7-8. Drawings by Steve Dawson.

Figure 7-9. Drawings by Tracy Steszyn and Christina Jams.

Figure 7-10. Drawings by Steve Dawson.

Figure 7-13. [Fish] M. C. Escher. Reprinted by permission of Cordon Art.

Figure 7-18. Drawing by Lyda Kobylansky.

Figure 7-19. Drawing by Henry Furmanowicz.

Figure 7-20. Drawing by Lyda Kobylansky.

Figure 7-21. Drawing by Nick Zannella.

Figure 7-22. Drawings by Steve Dawson and Henry Furmanowicz.

Figure 7-24. [Lizard I] M. C. Escher. Reprinted by permission of Cordon Art.

Figure 7-28. Drawing by Steve Dawson.

Figure 7-29. [Lizard II] M. C. Escher. Reprinted by permission of Cordon Art.

Figure 7-34. Drawings by Steve Dawson.

Figure 7-35. *Study of Regular Division of the Plane with Reptiles*. M. C. Escher. 1939. Pencil, india ink, and watercolor. (Used for the lithograph *Reptiles*.) Reprinted by permission of Cordon Art.

Figure 7-39. Drawing by Steve Dawson.

Figure 7-40. [Birds] M. C. Escher. Reprinted by permission of Cordon Art.

Figure 7-43. "Tisha" by Stephen Makris.

Figure 7-44. Drawings by Steve Dawson.

Figure 7-45. [Lizard IV] M. C. Escher. Reprinted by permission of Cordon Art.

Figure 7-49. *Metamorphosis [I]*. M. C. Escher. May 1937. Woodcut. Reprinted by permission of Cordon Art.

Figure 7-50. *Study of Regular Division of the Plane with Human Figures*. M. C. Escher. 1936. Pencil and watercolor. (Used for the woodcut *Metamorphosis I*, 1937.) Reprinted by permission of Cordon Art.

Figure 7-55. [Crabs] M. C. Escher. Reprinted by permission of Cordon Art.

Figure 7-58. Drawing by Steve Dawson.

Figure 7-59. [Dogs] M. C. Escher. Reprinted by permission of Cordon Art.

Figure 7-63. *Study of Regular Division of the Plane with Human Figures*. M. C. Escher. 1944. Pencil and india ink. (Used for the lithograph *Encounter*, 1944.) Reprinted by permission of Cordon Art.

Figure 7-65. *Study of Regular Division of the Plane with Birds*. M. C. Escher. 1955. India ink and watercolor. (Used for the wood engraving *Swans*, 1956.) Reprinted by permission of Cordon Art.

Figure 7-69. Drawings by Steve Dawson.

Figure 7-70. *Study of Regular Division of the Plane with Horsemen*. M. C. Escher. 1946. India ink and watercolor. (Used for woodcut *Horseman*, 1946.) Reprinted by permission of Cordon Art.

Figure 7-74. Drawing by Sheila LeBlanc.

Students and Teachers:

Enter Our Third

TESSELLATION ART CONTEST

Win Dale Seymour Publications Merchandise

See Your Tessellation in Print!

Winners will receive a copy of a book featuring the
winning designs, as well as a copy of *Introduction to
Tessellations* by Dale Seymour and Jill Britton. The top
winners will also receive a $50 gift certificate for
merchandise carried by Dale Seymour Publications.

Contest Rules on Reverse

Contest Rules

1. Each entry must be submitted on two sheets of unlined 8½-by-11-inch white paper.

2. On the first sheet, draw the generating polygon with modifying curves superimposed in their appropriate locations. Modifying curves may be transformed by any of these procedures: translation, rotation, reflection, and glide reflection. The resulting shape should not exceed 3 inches in diameter in any direction. Do not show added details on this first sheet.

3. On the second sheet, show the completed tessellation with interior details added. Make all markings with black ink, lead pencil, or a computer printer. Do not use color or pencil shading.

4. All drawings must be the original work of a teacher or of a student enrolled in one of the grades K–12 or college on the submission date.

5. Computer-generated entries will be judged separately from hand-drawn designs.

6. Mail entries, **along with a completed entry form,** by June 30, 1994, to TESSELLATION ART CONTEST, Dale Seymour Publications, P.O. Box 10888, Palo Alto, CA 94303. Keep a copy of the submitted artwork.

7. By submitting your artwork, you agree that all rights in that artwork, including all copyrights, are assigned to and become the property of Dale Seymour Publications, and shall be considered "work made for hire" under the copyright act. Entries cannot be returned.

8. For a list of winners, send a self-addressed stamped envelope, Attention: Tessellation Contest Winners, after October 1, 1994.

Sample Entry

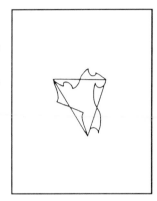

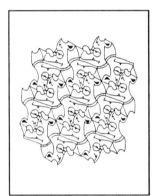

- -

Entry Form

Name _____

Grade_____ (the grade you are now in or have most recently completed)

School_____ Teacher_____

School Address _____

Home Address_____

I verify that this is my original artwork, and I understand that it will become the property of Dale Seymour Publications as a "work made for hire" under the copyright act.

Signature_____

Parent's Signature _____
   (student and parent or guardian must both sign for students under 18 years of age)

For teachers of students submitting artwork: I give permission for my name to accompany this student's artwork if it appears in forthcoming Dale Seymour Publications material.

Teacher's Signature _____